a

COLLOQUIAL
HINDUSTANI

COLLOQUIAL HINDUSTANI

By

A. H. HARLEY, M.A., I.E.S. (Retd.)

*Lecturer in Hindustani in the School of Oriental and
African Studies, University of London*

With an Introduction by

J. R. FIRTH, M.A.

*Reader in Linguistics and Indian Phonetics in the University
of London, at the School of Oriental and African Studies*

LONDON

KEGAN PAUL, TRENCH, TRUBNER & CO. LTD.

BROADWAY HOUSE: 68–74 CARTER LANE, E.C.

First published 1944

Printed in Great Britain by T. and A. CONSTABLE LTD,
at the University Press, Edinburgh

CONTENTS

PREFACE

COLLOQUIAL HINDUSTANI is intended to supply the beginner in the language not only with the common rules of grammar and their exemplification with sentences of a practical nature, but to assist him towards a correct pronunciation, with a phonetic system of spelling designed as part of an All-India system of romanic orthography, by Mr. J. R. Firth, Reader in Linguistics and Indian Phonetics in the University of London, at the School of Oriental and African Studies.

The compiler desires to acknowledge with deep gratitude his indebtedness to Mr. Firth for providing the Alphabet and the Introduction, and for reading through the entire manuscript and suggesting numerous improvements. His critical judgment has generously helped in various ways.

Mr. Rafiq Anwar (Aligarh University) has kindly co-operated by revising the translations, and has enhanced the practical utility of the book by supplying several pages of colloquial sentences on matters connected with office routine, travel and radio, and conversation on the telephone.

This collaboration makes it possible to submit this little book with a certain amount of confidence in its serviceability to the reader.

A. H. HARLEY.

January 1943.

INTRODUCTION

I. GENERAL

HINDUSTANI, like Bengali, Marathi, Gujerati and most other Indian languages except those of the south-eastern part of the peninsula, has its ancient origins in the Prakrits or "vernaculars" associated with Sanskrit. The widespread common language Hindustani is closely associated with two specialised literary languages, Hindi and Urdu. Hindi, written from left to right in the Devanagari or Sanskrit alphabet, borrows largely from Sanskrit. Urdu, written from right to left in an adapted form of the Persi-Arabic script brought by the Muslim invaders from over the North-West frontier, is naturally full of loan words from Persian and Arabic. Still, Urdu and Hindi are " of one language " with Hindustani and the other Sanskritic languages of India. Through the well-known relationship of Sanskrit, Persian, Greek, and Latin, they belong, with most of the languages of Europe, to the great linguistic family usually called Indo-European.

The everyday speech of well over fifty million people of all communities in the North of India is the expression of a common language, Hindustani. This language is shared at different levels and in varying degrees by about fifty million more in the North, in Hyderabad Deccan and in all parts of India. Growing steadily, this vast language community of close on a hundred million people is the third largest in the world, coming next after Chinese and English.

People who speak Hindustani may read and write Urdu in the adapted Persian character, or Hindi in the Devanagari (Sanskrit) character, or indeed both. But the cultural specialisation of the two languages emphasised by the two different scripts divides people whenever the common social life is either predominantly Muslim, or predominantly Hindu. In such circumstances one highly specialised form of spoken Hindustani would, if written down, normally appear in the Urdu script, another in the Hindi script. The speakers quite naturally would claim to be speaking Urdu or speaking Hindi. The simple, common speech of everyday life, however, might equally well áppear in either script. The truth is that the basic common language of many millions of Indians of Hindustani speech has no written form common to all. That is why people hesitate to recognise Hindustani as a language.

In this book Hindustani is presented as a language with an " orthography " of its own. This " orthography," though romanic in form, is thoroughly Indian both phonetically and linguistically, as every speaker of Hindustani will at once recognise. It forms an organic part of a consistent scheme for an All-India alphabet [1] designed on linguistic principles for the main languages of India entirely from the Indian point of view.

In this simple romanic orthography, Hindustani, though appearing in clothes of a new design, is still dressed in a national costume which fits it well, whereas in the usual European transliterations and transcriptions bristling with dots, dashes, and other diacritical marks, which do not really belong to the letters, it looks like a man who has lost his own clothes and has to make shift with an ill-fitting borrowed suit, pinned up here, let down there. To remove the pins and drop the fussy alterations, leaving Hindustani in the bare roman alphabet, is a great temptation to the European. And we know that the dots and dashes do, in fact, tend to wear off. The feeling that diacritics are extraneous to the roman alphabet is very strong indeed among people who do not require them. It is a sound instinct.

Unfortunately the bare unaltered roman alphabet is inadequate for the representation of Indian languages. So much so, that when this is attempted the result is sometimes as much as thirty to forty per cent. " illiterate." Certain publications in " Roman Urdu " (*sic*) issued under the auspices of the Government of India unfortunately fall into that category. " Illiteracy " of this kind, in cold print, is no way to promote " literacy " among the Indian peasantry or spread enlightenment among the half-educated.

---

[1] The All-India alphabet is also used in the first part of Miss H. M. Lambert's *Marathi Language Course* (Oxford University Press, Bombay).

See also *The Problem of a National Script for India*, by Professor Daniel Jones. Obtainable in England from Stephen Austin & Sons, Hertford, price 6d., or in India from The Pioneer Press, Lucknow, U.P., price 4 annas.

The alternative is the addition of a minimum number of extra letters of roman type, already well established, enabling us to frame a consistent Indian alphabet. The Indian roman alphabet then takes its proper place in grammars and dictionaries. A grammatical roman spelling is established, in which all Indians can practise literacy without shame, and which opens the door to easier learning of Indian languages by foreigners of all the continents. It is the method followed in this book.

The main advantages of this romanic spelling for the foreign learner are ease and speed of learning which make for early fluency. A fair pace of delivery in reading is possible from the start and transition to the Indian scripts is also facilitated, as will be seen from the tables on pages xxvii ff., which show that the All-India alphabet is based on similar phonetic principles to the Indian systems of writing.

The spelling is very broadly based on pronunciations widely accepted in Northern India between Lucknow and Lahore with Delhi as the normal centre.

In India, modern Indian languages are still unfortunately called " vernaculars," and instruction for Europeans is dominated by the " munshi " tradition. Some of the more recent " munshi " manuals have undoubtedly shown progress—but the age of munshiji, alas, will rapidly pass away after the war. The study and teaching of modern Indian languages in Europe is only just beginning to outgrow the Fort William tradition built up during the first half of last century. Most manuals of Hindustani introduce you to an India long gone by, a nostalgia for which continues to ache in the hearts of a few of the older lovers of India. A glance at the usual books will convince you that they have little contact with the age of steam and none with the age of electricity, oil, or of Dominion status.

This little book, and certain others, make a small beginning, especially in the matter of roman spelling, in what I hope will be a thorough-going overhaul of our text-books in Indian languages ; for history now moves at four hundred miles an hour, and India, already a progressive modern State of enormous potentialities, is destined to step again into the front rank in the Asia of to-morrow.

To get on well with the Hindustan of to-morrow, we shall need more speakers of Hindustani than we have ever had before.

II. PRONUNCIATION

Vowels

In speaking Received Standard English you use twenty-one different vowel sounds. In speaking Hindustani you need only *ten* different basic vowel sounds, but you must be able to nasalise all ten of them, and also to aspirate or " breathify " them. So that though Hindustani has only about half as many vowels as English, it trebles its means of differentiating words, by nasalisation and by breathiness.

The ten normal vowels are :—

ə	a	y	i	w	u	e	əy	o	əw
1	2	3	4	5	6	7	8	9	10

The first six simple vowels present very little difficulty to the English speaker, since they fall into three pairs—

> ə and a,   y and i,   w and u ;

y and i being rather like the English short and long vowels in the words *bid* and *bead*, and w and u roughly equivalent to the short and long vowels in *full* and *fool*. But the difference of length in Hindustani is not great, the important difference being the difference of vowel quality.

The three pairs of simple vowels :

1. ə.

This so-called short vowel is rather like what is called the neutral vowel in English. It sounds rather like the first vowel in *arise*, or the vowel in *but*. The Hindustani word səb (*all*) is more like the first syllable of *subject* (verb) than *subject* (noun). It is the so-called inherent vowel used in pronouncing the names of the consonant syllables in the Hindi alphabet, e.g. :

> kə,   khə,   gə,   ghə.   (See p. xxvii.)

2. a.

The so-called long vowel of the pair ə-a. Rather like the *a* in *father*. kam (*work*) sounds rather like the Yorkshire pronunciation of *calm*.

Examples of vowels ə and a :

    səlam, kəm, kam, səb, nam, lam, jəb, əb, ana, jana, ajana, bazar, jənab, pənjab, ag, aj, əgər, məgər, ləgna, kərna, ap, əpna, bəna, səkna, bənana, əfsər, nəmbər, sər, sara, pəlna, palna.

3. y.

Not very different from the Standard English pronunciation of vowels represented by *i* or *y* in *bid, sit, system, mystery*.

4. i.

Like the vowel sound in *seem, cease*, or in the second syllable of *immediately*, only without any trace of diphthongisation.

Examples of vowels y and i :

    dyn, din, ys, yn, jys, jyn, ky, ki, li, di, pysna, pisna, mim, sin, nim, byjli, myli, pynsyl, sahyb, əlyf, ytni, pina, pylana, jytna, jitna.

5. w.

Like the Standard pronunciation of the vowels in *put, foot*.

6. u.

Not very different from the Standard English vowel in *too, root, moodily*, without diphthongisation.

Examples of vowels w and u :

    ws, wn, upər, bwra, swna, hua, wmr, hwkm, rwkna, wrdu, talu, faltu, pwrana, pura, malum, dusra, dwkan, pwl, phul, bylkwl, skul, zəruri.

The more difficult vowels : e, əy, o, əw.

    e and əy may be paired as half-close and half-open front vowels, and o and əw as analogous half-close and half-open back vowels. It will be noticed that the symbols əy and əw are digraphs, although in ordinary colloquial pronunciation in Delhi and Lahore both əy and əw are simple vowels rather like the Southern English vowels in *had* and *nod*. The diphthongal pronunciation produced by gliding from Hindustani ə to y (not a to y) and from ə to w (not a to w), more common in Lucknow and farther East, is, however, covered by this spelling. The learner is strongly recommended to adopt the easier and equally acceptable pronunciation as simple vowels, whereas if he tries the difficult diphthongal pronunciation, he will in all probability perpetrate the foreign and somewhat ridiculous pronunciation of həy as *high*, and nəw (9) as *now*. The latter pronunciation in any case suggests the entirely different word nao, or nav, meaning *boat*. If the student learns to avoid the " *high* " pronunciation of həy (*is*), he will be helping to remove one of the most recurrent howlers of " English " Hindustani.

7. e.

A pure or simple vowel something like the Italian and other continental values of " e " ; a vowel quality somewhere between the Scottish and North of England vowels in such words as *made, grey, ace*, and not at all like the London diphthong in such words. In Southern English perhaps some people approach it in the very slight diphthong represented by the " a " in *cessation* or *lately*.

8. əy.

The very common word həy (*is*) is rather like the beginning of the Southern English word *ham* ; it is the South Country *ham* or Northern *hem* stopping short just before the " m." The English word *lamp* is borrowed as ləymp.

9. o.

Like e, it is a pure vowel of the Continental, Scottish, or Northern English type. Some English people use a short " o " of this type in words like *November* and *phonetics*.

In practising e and o, keep the tongue and lip positions steady and the lower jaw fixed—no chin movement, no lip diphthong.

N.B.—The vowels a, i, e, o in *final* position are grammatically significant. In final position they are fairly short, but their qualities must be kept, and not relaxed or lowered to ə, y, əy, or əw. ai, ae, əi, əe, and əy must be kept distinct.

Examples of vowels e and o :

    roz, bolo, lena, sona, bona, gora, ek, do, ae, ao (cf. ai), gəe, jo, ho, hoga, hoge, lelo, dedo, mez, rel, goli, rəhoge, jao, pao, mom, log, lie, ləgega.

10. əw.

Rather like the vowel in Southern English *nod* without outer lip-rounding. It must *not* sound like the Southern English vowel in *gnawed*, though the Yorkshire vowel in that word would not be so bad. It must *never* be pronounced like the vowel in English *how, now*.

Examples of vowels əy and əw :

həy, məyl, səw, nəw, jəwn, kəwn, jəysa, həyza, əwr, əwrət, gəya, nəya, nəwkər, bəwna, səyr, səynma.

Nasalisation and Aspiration of the Ten Vowels:

	1	2	3	4	5	6	7	8	9	10
Normal :	ə	a	y	i	w	u	e	əy	o	əw
Nasalised :	əŋ	aŋ	yŋ	iŋ	wŋ	uŋ	eŋ	əyŋ	oŋ	əwŋ
h-coloured or Aspirated	əh	ah	yh	ih	wh	uh	eh	əyh	oh	əwh

Nasalisation.

The nasalisation of vowels has always been a feature of the Sanskritic languages. It is called ənwnasyk [1] (" accompanied by nasality ") and has a special sign, which is rendered in this spelling by ŋ immediately after the vowel to be nasalised. Thus, aŋ and oŋ stand for nasalised a and nasalised o, being rather like the French syllables *an* and *on* (ã and õ). The nasalisation of the vowel of həy (*is*) gives the plural həyŋ (*are*). The ŋ in such words as həyŋ is not a consonant and must not be pronounced like the "ng" in *hang*. The vowel in həyŋ is quite like the Southern English vowel in *hang*, but the nasal part is mixed with or accompanies the vowel, as in the French interjection " *hein!* "

Aspiration.

The aspiration of vowels is indicated by h immediately after the vowel which has a breathy quality, or is " h "-coloured especially at the end, rather like the " sighing out " of *ah!* The exclamatory syllables *ah!* and *oh!* in English can be pronounced either with " bright " voice using a minimum of breath, or " breathily " quite in the Indian manner.

[1] ənwnasyk being here differentiated from ənwsvar (nasal after-sound) which includes consonantal nasals.

Examples of nasalised and aspirated vowels :

həyŋ, kəhaŋ (compare həy and kəha), məyŋ, meŋ, ynhoŋ, huŋ, haŋ, vəhaŋ, yəhaŋ, nəhiŋ, gərmioŋ, gyreŋ, gyruŋga, logoŋ, kəreŋge, nəwkəroŋ, aŋkheŋ, paŋc, həŋsna, maŋgna, pəyhle, yeh, voh,[1] kəyhna, rəyhna, bəyhra (cf. bəyra), mehtər, mehman, cahna.

In words like bəyhs and bəwht the closing aspiration of the vowel is followed by a short echo of the same vowel just before the final consonant, giving the impression of two syllables, the second being a very short echo of the vowel in the first. bəwht (*very*) must *not* be pronounced like *boat* or *bought*.

Nasalisation and aspiration may be combined, as in the first syllable of pəwhŋcna. Of the three possibilities pəhwŋcna, pəwhŋcna, pəwŋhcna, the second is adopted in this book, but it does not really matter which spelling is adopted, ŋh or hŋ.

Other examples are meŋh, muŋh.

The names of the ten vowel signs are the same as their pronunciation in isolation. The name of the nasalisation sign ŋ is əŋ, and of the vowel-aspirate h, əh. əh must be distinguished from the consonantal aspirate h which is called hə. In the consonantal digraphs kh, gh, ph, bh, etc., the h is part of the twin symbols which are called khə, ghə, etc.

CONSONANTS

On the whole Hindustani is an easy language to learn, but the correct pronunciation of the consonants is difficult for all foreigners, and not only for Englishmen. A few Englishmen have, nevertheless, learnt to speak Hindustani quite like Indians, in spite of our almost traditional neglect of the backbone of the language, which is what may be called the Indian consonant system.

Hindustani requires a minimum of 31 consonantal distinctions to be maintained in speech, in addition to the two semi-vowels. If the pronunciation is to be applied to Urdu, then four more (q, x, ɣ, and ʒ) must be added, making 35 without the semivowels y and v. English requires only 20 consonants, and of these only 9 (b, g, m, n, s, z, ʃ, ʒ, and h) could safely be equated with Indian sounds. So that Englishmen have to go out of their way to practise at least 22 of the consonant sounds of Hindustani, *not* including the 4 non-Indian sounds of Urdu, q, x, ɣ, and ʒ, for which k, kh, g, j, or z are regularly substituted by Indians themselves.

[1] See footnote on p. xxx.

Consonant Table

			Velar Back of tongue and soft palate	Palatal Front of tongue and front part of hard palate. Tip down	Retroflex Edge or rim of tongue behind or on teeth ridge	Dental Tip of tongue touches upper teeth	Bi-labial and labio-dental
PLOSIVES	Voiceless	Unasp.	k	c	ṭ	t	p
		Asp.	kh	ch	ṭh	th	ph
	Voiced	Unasp.	g	j	ḍ	d	b
		Asp.	gh	jh	ḍh	dh	bh
NASALS						n	m
FRICATIVES	Voiceless		x (kh)	ʃ	—	Alveolar s	f
	Voiced		ɣ (g)	[ʒ]	—	z	—
Flapped and tapped sounds			—	—	ɽ	r	—
Uvular plosive (Arabic)			q (k)	—	aspirated ɽh	—	—
Aspirate, semi-vowels and liquid			h	y	—	l	v

The main difficulties of pronunciation lie in the plosive consonants. Special attention should be paid to the first and fourth horizontal columns of the table of plosives. English speakers will have considerable difficulty with the unaspirated voiceless series k, c, ṭ, t, p, even in final position, while of the voiced plosives, on the other hand, it is the aspirated series gh, jh, ḍh, dh, bh which require considerable practice, especially in initial position. Of the vertical columns the central matter of prime importance is the difference of articulation between retroflex and dental, i.e. between the series ṭ, ṭh, ḍ, ḍh, and the series t, th, d, dh. Not until these characteristic differences are habitually maintained will the pronunciation sound at all like Hindustani. When they are, the speaker will have established a command of the consonantal backbone, not only of Hindustani, but also of Marathi, Gujerati, Bengali and a number of other Indian languages. Mastery of the twenty plosives is the key to a good Indian pronunciation. Neglect them, and however skilful you may imagine you are with x, ɣ, and q, you will not even approximate to a minimum of phonetic courtesy.

The table of plosives containing five columns of four each presents the consonantal backbone of the language, and indeed of all the Sanskritic languages of India. It is to be noted that though the aspirated plosives are represented by digraphs or twin letters, they are phonetically single efforts and single units, represented in the Sanskrit alphabet by their own letters, which, as will be seen from the table on p. xxvii, bear no resemblance to the letters for the unaspirated sounds.

The outstanding difficulties for the great majority of foreign learners are :

(i) The two so-called " t " and " d " sounds,
ṭ, t; ḍ, d.

(ii) The five unaspirated voiceless plosives, especially c and t.

(iii) The five aspirated voiced plosives,
gh, jh, ḍh, dh, bh.

(iv) Double consonants.

(v) The retroflex flapped ṛ (perhaps most difficult of all).

The first and most important step in learning to pronounce Hindustani is to distinguish between the retroflex series ṭ, ṭh, ḍ, ḍh and the dental series t, th, d, dh. All speakers of Hindustani, of whatever dialect, maintain these distinctions. Except Assamese, all the main Indian languages require the distinction ṭ and t, generally ignored by Englishmen, who fuss about x or q which do not matter, and neglect the central features which matter very much to hundreds of millions of Indians.

Aspirated and Unaspirated Voiceless Consonants:

Most speakers of Southern English release *p*, *t*, and *k* with a slight aspiration in initial position in a stressed syllable and also finally—e.g. *peak, tack, coat, tap*, though immediately after " s " the aspiration is not noticeable—e.g. *speak, stack*; unaspirated plosives also occur between vowels in such words as *sipping, knitting, knocking*. In Hindustani, k, c, ṭ, t, p are released with a minimum of breath. There must be no outward puff of breath from the lungs. To understand this, practise p and k while holding your breath. You may produce a sort of " popping " explosion of " p." That is the basis. Eliminate the audible pop, and you have an unaspirated p. The opposite action of leaving your throat open for freely flowing breath enables you to produce ph, kh, etc., which have a good strong outflow of breath when the lips part, often assisted by a push from the diaphragm at the instant of release. ph is not really like the junction of *p* and *h* in *tophat*, it is one effort, a " p "-sound in which you forcibly " spit out " the aspiration, phu!

i. (*a*). ṭ.

The main thing in the production of this and the other retroflex sounds is not *where* you touch the teeth ridge or just behind it, but *how* you touch it. In fact the place of articulation is just about where most of us make the " t " of *try* or *true*. The Indian ṭ, however, is not made with the tip in the English manner, but with the very edge or rim of the tip, which is slightly curled back to make this possible, almost as when you have to hold an elusive pill on the end of your tongue to prevent it from going down or rolling off. As one would expect, English " t " and " d " are replaced by Hindustani ṭ and ḍ in loan words such as :

motər, steʃən, mastər, mystər, ṭykyṭ, sygrəṭ, ṭrəym, ṭrəwlibəs, ḍrəyvər, ṭəyksi, ḍaktər, ḍyuṭi, pəyḍ, koṭ, bətən, soḍa, ṭelifun, reḍyo, propəgənḍa, ḍrama, ḍaynyng hal, hosṭəl, yunyvərsṭi.

i. (*b*). t.

Unlike ṭ, the dental t is pronounced with a flat tongue, the edges touching the inside of the upper teeth all round. A safe way of learning it, is to make sure the tip of the tongue touches the cutting edge of the front teeth. Some English people use a dental " t " in *eighth*, and in *at* when followed by *th* in such phrases as *at the theatre, at three, at thirty*. Compare this variety of English " t " with the " t " in *true*, which is nearer the Hindustani ṭ.

Having established the articulation of ṭ and t, English speakers will find it easier to begin with the aspirated ṭh and th. Note that -ta corresponds grammatically to the English verbal ending " *ing* " and is very common, and tha=*was* (m. s.).

Examples of ṭ, ṭh, t, th :

voh ata həy (*he comes*)   voh roti həy (*she weeps*)
voh aṭa həy (*that is flour*)   voh roṭi həy (*that is bread*)

tana, thana, ṭhana, ṭəkna, thəkna, wtna, wṭhna, tapna, thapna, ṭhik, koṭ, koṭhi, sat, sath, saṭh, ata tha, ati thi, ate the, kaṭa, khata, pəta, phəṭa, piṭ, piṭh, beṭa, bəyṭha, mata, matha.

ii. c, ch, j, jh.

The most difficult of the unaspirated plosives is c, which is pronounced with the tip of the tongue down, behind the lower teeth. If you try to pronounce " ty " with the tip of the tongue down and without any aspiration, you will get some idea of the sound. The English *ch* in *church* will do for the aspirated ch of Hindustani, but is a bad beginning for c. Similarly the English *j* in *judge* will do for jh in such words as bwjhna, səməjhna, or in phrases like mwjh ko, but it is a bad beginning for Hindustani j which, as the voiced correlate of c, is much more like a " dy " sound pronounced with the tip of the tongue down and with a minimum of friction on release. Scarcely any fricative release is audible in bəjna, whereas there is a good deal in bwjhna.

Examples of c, ch, j, jh.

ciz, cyṭṭhi, car, paṇc, chəy, jana, jata, bəca, mwjhe, səmjha, becna, jəcna, bychna, bəcana, bychana, pucha, chuna, cuna, cwna, cahna, cahta, chaṇṭa, caṭa, chata, kuc, kwch.

iii. The Aspirated Voiced Plosives : gh, jh, ḍh, dh, bh.

These are the voiced correlates of kh, ch, ṭh, th, and ph, and
fundamentally are produced in the same way, with forcible
"spitting out" of the *voiced* breath. They are easy enough
between vowels, not quite so easy finally and quite difficult at
the beginning of a word. Various ways of learning these may
be tried, though the usual suggestions of *log-house, road-house*
(for ḍh), *cab-horse* (for bh) do not really approximate to the
action required. To get bh this way, you must divide the
syllables in a very un-English way, e.g. *ho-bhouse*. A variant
of this is to say hab-hab-hab-hab-ha—bha—bha. You begin by
saying hab-hab-hab, and speed up the linking so that you con-
vert it to a repetition of bha bha, etc. Another way is to regard
the b part of bh merely as a closed lip position from which you
are going to "spit out" ha, which you have all ready inside
under pressure, so to speak. The ha part begins with a voiced h.

N.B.—bəhai and bhai are two quite different words, the second
one having only *one* syllable, similarly in the following pairs.

bəhai, bhai, bəhar, bhar, bəhana, bhana, bəhao, bhao, bəhi,
bhi, bhəi.

Examples of the Voiced Plosives, aspirated and unaspirated :
bənd, baŋdhna, bag, bhag, bagh, gyrna, ghyrna, gora, ghər,
gyn, ghyn, gyddh, gwl, ghwlgəya, əndər, ydhər, wdhər,
aŋdhi, do, dona, dhona, dhaŋp, dhaŋk, ḍak, ḍher, der,
ḍhai, aj, jo, jəb, jal, jhal, jəṭ, jhəṭ, sujna, sujhna, səməjh,
səmaj, bhuna, bwna, bhulna, bolna, bwdh, kəbhi, lobh.

iv. Double Consonants.

The doubling of consonant sounds is not very common in
English. We do, however double the " n "-sound in words like
unknown, unnecessary, and some people use a double " l "-sound
in *wholely* to distinguish it from *holy*, with one " l "-sound. Similarly in Hindustani there are pairs like jana, janna, cwna, cwnna,
bəna, bənna, gəla, gəlla, pyla (or pyləw), and pylla. But these
are not all. The distinction between single and double consonant sounds must be maintained throughout. For example,
the double k in pəkka is rather like the long " k "-sound in
book-case, the double ṭ in pəṭṭha might be suggested by the long
" t "-sound in *hot-tea*.

Examples of plosive consonants to illustrate doubling and other characteristics dealt with above :

pəta, pəṭa, pətta, pəṭṭa, pəṭṭha, phəṭa, phəṭṭa, pətthər, təṭṭi, ḍybbi, həḍḍi, bəca, bəcca, bəta, bhətta, sətər, səttər, myṭi, myṭṭi, cəkkər, mwrəbba, ḷwcca, ləccha, gwccha, ḍhəka, dhəkka, məkkhi, məkka, kəṭa, khəṭṭa, kəta, kətha, kəttha.

Other examples of doubling : rəssi, hyssa, əmma, təlləffwz.

Certain sequences of different plosives are especially difficult : e.g. ṭ, t, and th, as in phəṭta tha, bəyṭhta tha.

v. ṛ.

The retroflex flapped ṛ is perhaps the most difficult Indian sound for a foreigner to acquire, and very few indeed learn to flap it as quickly as an Indian. It is interesting to note that both the Muslims and Europeans think of it as a sort of " r "-sound, whereas to most Indians it is a very rapidly flapped " ḍ " occurring chiefly between vowels. It does not occur initially. The body of the tongue is withdrawn with the blade curled back as for ḍ or ṭ (see p. xix). Having your teeth apart, try to point towards the back of your mouth with the tip of the tongue, but do not touch anywhere. From that position the blade is flicked forward and down, the tip finishing up behind the lower teeth. Before the flap takes place the underneath of the blade can be seen, and when the sound is made a very rapid flick of the under edge of the tip catches the gums as it flaps past.

It also occurs aspirated, ṛh.

r.

This is a tapped " r," one or two taps being usual. Some English people used a tapped " r " in such words as *three, barren, quarrel.* When doubled it sounds like a long-rolled or trilled " r." The Southern English fricative " r " just passes muster, but is not a sound to keep, if the aim is good pronunciation.

Examples of r, rr, ṛ, ṛh :

bwra, bəṛa, toṛa, thoṛa, gora, ghoṛa, pəhaṛ, phaṛ, gəṛi, ghəṛi, gaṛi, gaṛhi, pəṛhna, pər, pəṛh, baṛh, bhaṛ, khari, kaṛhi, kərna, kəṛhna, kərra, kəṛa, khəṛa, kəṛi, khəṛi, khəri, kəṛhi, ləṛai.

N.B.—English speakers will have some difficulty in pronouncing a final r preceded by a vowel, especially i and u. In Southern English the title Amir sounds like *a mere*, and rhymes with *beer*. There is no final " r." In Hindustani you must hang on to the clear i to the very instant the tapped r is made. There must be no neutral or glide vowel between the i and the r. Similarly with other vowels.

E.g. pir, dur, der, mohr are not at all like Southern English *peer, doer, dare, moor* or *more*. pər is not at all like Southern English *purr*, though the Scottish pronunciation would be near it. Similarly kər is the Scots " *cur* "; kərta does *not* rhyme with English *curter*. Having no " er "-sound, Scots sometimes say *kernel* for *colonel* ; quite similarly the Hindustani for *colonel* is kərnəyl.

n. For all practical purposes the English " n " will do. But it must be remembered that when n immediately precedes one of the plosive consonants it takes on the articulation of that consonant. Before the k-series, n is pronounced like the so-called English " *ng* "-sound ; in fact as it is in English in such words as *think, finger*, e.g. :

ənk, əng, rəng, nənga, bəynk, ṭəynk.

When followed by the c-series it is palatal, having a tip-down articulation like the consonant following, e.g. :

pənc, pənchi, ənjən, pənjab.

Similarly, n is retroflex in ənḍa, kənṭh, ṭənṭa, bənṭa, ghənṭa, and dental in bənd, əndər, kənt, kəntha.

l. Always a clear " i "-like " l," as in Southern English at the beginning of such words as *lee, leaf*, but *never* as in *feel* or *field*. English speakers must go out of their way to pronounce a clear " l " in such words as pwl, phul, myl, mil, which are not at all like English *pull, pool, mill, meal*. Nor is the l of mwlk at all like the " l " of *milk*. Americans and Western Scots will find l difficult, Frenchmen and Germans easy.

The Semi-vowels y and v.

y. It is really a very short form of the vowel y, and is much less " consonantal " than in English. Indians do not properly pronounce the " y " sound after the " b " which distinguishes *beauty* from *booty*. ḍyuṭi is in fact very different from the English pronunciation of *duty*. y is tenser and closer after i, e.g. təiyar, gəvəiya.

v. Similarly v is much more of a vowel than a consonant. It has all the back or " *oo* " quality of w, but no lip rounding. The middle only of the lower lip *barely* touches the middle of the upper teeth. Even when doubled there is no audible friction, e.g. qwvvət, əvvəl.

For m, f, s, z, ʃ, ʒ, h an English pronunciation will serve all practical purposes. The special symbol ʃ is necessary for the " sh "-sound, since s-h, as in the English word *mis-hap*, occur consecutively. ʒ is the sibilant in *pleasure* and occurs in a very few loan words of Persian origin. Many Indians substitute j for z and ʒ.

Only three consonant sounds remain, x, ɣ, and q, which occur in Arabic and Persian loan words and are necessary for a good Delhi and Lucknow pronunciation of that type of Hindustani which links up with Urdu. Many Indian speakers of Hindustani substitute kh, g, and k for x, ɣ, and q, so that foreigners may do the same if they do not aim at good Urdu-Hindustani.

x. x is like what we call the " *ch* "-sound of *loch*, or the " *ach* "-sound of German, only rather further back and more " scrapy."

ɣ. ɣ is the voiced correlate of x, made in a similar way. Rather like the " rubbing " pronunciation of " *g* " in *wagen* by some Germans, but not trilled or rolled, and further back than the " back r " of German *waren*, or French *aurons*.

q. The furthest back " k "-sound you can make. To make it easier to close the opening at the back of the mouth with the back of the tongue against the uvula, it is necessary to squeeze the sides of the throat nearer together to narrow the opening.

Examples of x, ɣ, and q: k, kh and g:

kana, khana, xana, kali, khali, xali, təkta, təxta, kan, xan, bag, baɣ, baqi, baɣi, gwl, ghwl, ɣwl, gol, ghol, ɣol, rəkhna, rəxna, qərib, ɣərib, xylaf, ɣylaf, xəm, ɣəm, xəbər, qəbər (qəbr).

III. ACCENT

The strong stress accent of the Englishman completely distorts the rhythm of Hindustani, which ordinarily moves evenly within a narrower range of intonation. On the whole, the effect of English stress accent on Hindustani, coupled with the usual pronunciation howlers, is much worse than the average Indian performance in English. A great deal can be learnt by studying the accent of Northern Indians when speaking English.

A rough idea of the intonation of a simple phrase may be suggested by the following arrangement of syllables :

(*he is going*).

To some people the intonation of Hindustani suggests Welsh.

A Graphic Representation of Hindustani Intonation in Slow Speech

(One mark per syllable)

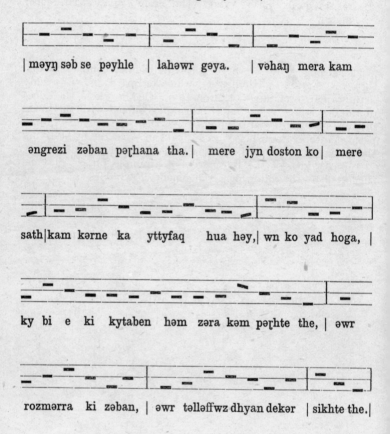

| məyŋ səb se pəyhle | lahəwr gəya. | vəhaŋ mera kam

əngrezi zəban pəɽhana tha. | mere jyn doston ko | mere

sath|kam kərne ka yttyfaq hua həy,| wn ko yad hoga, |

ky bi e ki kytaben həm zəra kəm pəɽhte the, | əwr

rozmərra ki zəban, | əwr təlləffwz dhyan dekər | sikhte the.|

IV. THE DEVANAGARI OR HINDI ALPHABET

(Cf. Table on p. xvii)

kə क़	cə च	ʈə ट	tə त	pə प
khə ख	chə छ	ʈhə ठ	thə थ	phə फ
gə ग	jə ज	ɖə ड	də द	bə ब
ghə घ	jhə झ	ɖhə ढ	dhə ध	bhə भ
			nə न	mə म
xə (khə) ख़	ʃə श		sə स	fə फ़
ɤə (gə) ग़	[ʒə]		zə ज़	
		ɽə ड़	rə र	
qə (kə) क़		ɽhə ढ़		
hə ह	yə य		lə ल	və व

1. Vowel Syllables :

ə	a	y	i	w	u	e	əy	o	əw	əŋ	əh
अ	आ	इ	ई	उ	ऊ	ए	ऐ	ओ	औ	अं	अः

2. Consonant-vowel Syllables :

kə	ka	ky	ki	kw	ku	ke
क	का	कि	की	कु	कू	के

kəy	ko	kəw	kəŋ	kəh
कै	को	कौ	कं	कः

Similarly throughout the syllabary.

Example :

məyŋ səb se pəyhle lahəwr gəya. vəhaŋ mera kam
मैं सब से पैहले लाहौर गया । वहां मेरा काम

əngrezi zəban pəṛhana tha. mere jyn doston ko mere
अंग्रेज़ी ज़बान पढ़ाना था । मेरे जिन दोस्तों को मेरे

sath kam kərne ka yttyfaq hua həy, wn ko yad hoga,
साथ काम करने का इत्तिफ़ाक़ हुआ है, उन को याद होगा,

ky bi e ki kytaben həm zəra kəm pəṛhte the, əwr
कि बी . ए . की किताबें हम ज़रा कम पढ़ते थे, और

rozmərra ki zəban, əwr tələffwz dhyan dekər sikhte the.
रोज़मर्रा की ज़बान, और तलफ़्फ़ुज़ ध्यान देकर सीखते थे ।

V. THE PERSI-ARABIC OR URDU ALPHABET

Initial											
Medial											
Final											
Detached form											
	ʻ y	f	q	k	g	l	m	n	v	h	y etc.
Name	ʻeyn	fe	qaf	kaf	gaf	lam	mim	nun	vao	he	ye

Initial											
Medial											
Final											
Detached form											
	z	r	ṛ	z	ʒ	s	ʃ	s	z	t	z
Name	zal	re	ṭe	ze	ʒe	sin	jim	svad	zvad	toe	zoe	eyn

Initial											
Medial											
Final											
Detached form											
	ə, etc.	b	p	t	ṭ	s	j	c	h	x	d	ḍ
Name	alyf	be	pe	te	ṭe	se	jim	ce	he	xe	dal	ḍal

te and toe, se, sin and svad, ze, zoe and zvad are not differentiated in pronunciation. ze, zoe, zvad and ʒe are often pronounced like jim. The five unnecessary letters are partly responsible for the foreigner's failure to distinguish te and ṭe, which is a cardinal error.

Vowels as follows:

Representation of vowels (*reading from right to left*):

mul	mwl	mil	myl	mal	məl
مُول	مُل	مِيل	مِل	مال	مَل

məwlvi	mol	məyl	mel
مَولْوِی	مول	مَیْل	میل

EXAMPLE OF URDU SCRIPT

(*Read from right to left*)

kam mera vəhaŋ   .gəya lahəwr pəyhle se səb məyŋ

میں سب سے پہلے لاہور گیا   وہاں میرا کام

mere ko doston jyn mere   .tha pəɽhana zəban əngrezi

انگریزی زبان پڑھانا تھا   میرے جن دوستوں کو میرے

,hoga yad ko wn ,həy hua yttyfaq ka kərne kam sath

ساتھ کام کرنے کا اتّفاق ہواہے اُن کو یاد ہوگا

əwr ,the pəɽhte kəm zəra həm kytaben ki e bi ky

کہ بی اے کی کتابیں ہم ذرا کم پڑھتے تھے اور

.the sikhte dekər dhyan təlləffwz əwr ,zəban ki rozmərra

روزمرّہ کی زبان اور تلفّظ دھیان دیکر سیکھتے تھے

---

[1] Footnote to p. xvi.

The quality of the h-coloured or "aitchified" vowels commonly used in speech is sometimes different from that suggested by the Indian spelling; e.g. **yeh** and **voh** for "*yyh*" and "*vwh*." In final position normal vowels are often heard in such cases: e.g. **ye, vo, ky.** It will be noticed on p. 86 that **bara** (12), **tera** (13), etc., are preferred to **barəh, terəh.**

LESSON I

NOUNS

GENDER.—There are only two genders, masculine and feminine; males are masculine, females feminine. A few words can be either masculine or feminine: e.g. nəwkər *servant*; dwʃmən, *enemy*; sathi, *companion*.

The following general rules will be serviceable, but do not suffice for all nouns:

Feminine are:

(*a*) Abstract nouns, names of lower animals, and lifeless matter in general, ending in **i**: e.g. xwʃi, *happiness*; jəldi, *quickness*.

Exceptions are: pani, *water*; ghi, *clarified butter*; ji, *mind*; dəhi, *curd*; hathi, *elephant*; moti, *pearl*—which are masculine.

(*b*) Nouns ending in **t** if derived from Arabic roots: e.g. rəyhmət, *mercy*; hərkət, *movement, action*.

(*c*) Nouns ending in -yʃ if derived from Persian verbal roots: e.g. pərəstyʃ, *sustenance*; vərzyʃ, *exercise*.

(*d*) There are many Arabic words formed on the pattern of təfil; all of them are feminine except taviz (*m.*), *amulet*.

Words ending in other letters are generally masculine.

N.B.—Where sex is indicated among the lower animals by a change of the final vowel from **a** to **i**, one of the two forms prevails for ready reference: e.g. a *dog* is referred to as kwtta, unless the *female*, kwtti, is specified; likewise a *horse* as ghoṛa; but a *cat* as bylli, and a *goat* as bəkri. There is no rule for guidance in the matter. nər and mada signify " *male* " and " *female* " respectively.

INFLECTION.—The various relationships of nouns, e.g. possessive, indirect object, etc., are expressed by means of certain terminal changes in the noun and the addition of certain particles known as Postpositions to these inflected forms.

A

Masculine nouns may for convenience be placed in two groups : (a) those ending in a consonant, or **i**, **u**, or **o** ; (b) those ending in a.

Group (a)

	Singular	Plural
Nominative or *Simple form.*	mərd (*man*)	mərd (*men*)
Inflected or *Oblique form.*	,,	mərdoŋ

With postpositions, added to the simple form in the singular and the oblique in the plural :

Singular

mərd ka,	*of a* (*the*) *man ; a* (*the*) *man's*
,, ko,	*to*	,,	,,	(also a form of the direct object)
,, meŋ,	*in*	,,	,,
,, se,	*from*	,,	,,
,, tək,	*up to*	,,	,,
,, ne	(Agent-sign)

Plural

mərdoŋ ka,	*of* (*the*) *men ;* (*the*) *men's*
,, ko,	*to*	,,	,,	(also a form of the direct object)
,, meŋ,	*in*	,,	,,
,, se,	*from*	,,	,,
,, tək,	*up to*	,,	,,
,, ne	(Agent-sign)

N.B.—(a) **ka** changes to **ki** and **ke** in the conditions stated at p. 4.

(b) **meŋ** means *in, among*; **pər**, *on, at*; **se**, *from, by, with*.

(c) **ne**, Agent-sign, see p. 33.

Group (b)

	Singular	Plural
Nominative.	ləṛka (*boy*)	ləṛke (*boys*)
Oblique.	ləṛke	ləṛkoŋ

Exceptions :—(1) pure Sanskrit words : e.g. **raja**, *ruler, king.*
(2) words denoting relatives : e.g. **cəca**, *paternal uncle* ; **dada**, *paternal grandfather.*
(3) Persian participial forms : e.g. **dana** (noun and adjective), *sage.*
(4) a number of foreign words : e.g. **xwda**, *God* ; **dərya**, *river* (Persian) ; **səhra**, *desert* (Arabic).

N.B.—These exceptions change only in the oblique plural : **dəryaoŋ meŋ**, *in rivers.*

Feminine nouns may conveniently be placed in three groups : (*a*) those ending in a consonant ; (*b*) those ending in **i** ; (*c*) diminutives ending in **ia**.

GROUP (*a*)

	Singular	*Plural*
Nominative.	**mez** (*table*)	**mezeŋ** (*tables*)
Oblique.	,,	**mezoŋ**

GROUP (*b*)

Nominative.	**ləɽki** (*girl*)	**ləɽkiaŋ**
Oblique.	,,	**ləɽkioŋ**

GROUP (*c*)

Nominative.	**cyɽia** (*small bird*)	**cyɽiaŋ** (*small birds*)
Oblique.	,,.	**cyɽioŋ**

N.B.—(*a*) In addressing or calling (vocative) the particle **əy**, *oh !* is used with the oblique form of the noun, but in the plural the ending is not nasalised : **əy ləɽke swno**, *boy, listen !* ; **əy ləɽko swno**, *boys, listen !* **ləɽka**, or **əy ləɽke**, **swn**, *boy, listen !* exemplifies the familiar use of the singular imperative (see p. 20).

(*b*) A plural-ending in **at** (in imitation of a certain Arabic feminine form) is added to some nouns ; the gender of the plural is generally that of its singular : **baɣat** (*m.*), *gardens* ; **təvəj-jwhat** (*f.*), *attentions.*

(*c*) There is no definite or indefinite article in the language. The place of an indefinite article is sometimes taken by the numeral **ek**, *one*, or the indefinite pronoun **koi**, *someone, a certain one* ; **ek admi** or **koi admi**, *a person.*

POSTPOSITIONS.—These all follow a noun in the oblique form, or the simple form if it cannot be inflected.

ka, or, as its position determines, **ki** or **ke**, the sign of possession, like the English *apostrophe s* ('*s*), stands between the possessor, which precedes it and is in the oblique form, and the possessed, with which it agrees in gender, number and form : **admi ka hath**, *the man's hand*. It changes, rather like an adjective (see p. 6), according to the following scheme :

| | *Singular* | | *Plural* | |
	Masc.	*Fem.*	*Masc.*	*Fem.*
Nom.	ka	ki	ke	ki
Obl.	ke	ki	ke	ki

In an expression such as " the dog belonging to Joseph's son " the Hindustani order of words would be : **yuswf ke beṭe ka kwtta**, *Joseph's son's dog*. In this **kwtta**, the last-possessed, is the keyword of the series ; the rule determining the form of **ka** has just been given ; all the words preceding it in the possessive relationship must be in the oblique.

ko :

(*a*) is the sign of the indirect object : **ləṛke ko ek rwpia do**, *give a rupee to the boy* ;

(*b*) it usually marks the definite direct object : **wstad ləṛkoŋ ko pəṛhata həy**, *the master teaches the boys* ;

(*c*) it is used with the oblique form of the noun in expressions of time and place : **somvar ko**, *on Monday* ; **dyn ko**, *by day* ; **adhi rat ko**, *at midnight* ; **kəlkətte ko jana**, *to go to Calcutta*—in time and place expressions it is often omitted : **wn dynoŋ**, *in those days* ; **kəlkətte jana**, *to go to Calcutta*.

meŋ, *in, among* : **ghəṛoŋ ke ehatoŋ meŋ**, *in the compounds of the houses.*

pər, *on, at* : **chət pər**, *on the roof* ; **ghər pər**, *at home.*

se, *from, by, with* : **xwʃi se**, *gladly* ; **zor se**, *by force* ; **bəṛhəi se mez bənvao**, *cause a table to be made by a carpenter.*

tək, *up to, until* ; zəmin se asman tək, *from earth to sky* ; sənicər tək, *till,* or *by, Saturday.* (*N.B.*—It has also the meaning of " even, including," but in this sense does not take the oblique form : ghoɽa tək vəhaŋ məwjud tha, *even the horse was there.*)

ne is added to the subject, i.e. the agent, when the Hindustani verb is transitive and in one of the past tenses (see p. 33).

VOCABULARY

ka kan, ear	*ka* sər, head
ka bal, hair	*ka* dərvaza, door
ka ghoɽa, horse	*ka* ghər, house
ka kam, work	*ki* zəban, tongue
ka swm, hoof	*ki* maŋ ; ma, mother
ka səvar, rider	*ki* dwm, tail
ka ʃer, tiger	*ki* əwrət, woman

N.B.—*ka* and *ki* are used throughout these lists to indicate masculine and feminine respectively, because these particles (generally called Postpositions) agree with a following noun in gender and number, in the manner of articles in French or adjectives in Hindustani.

EXAMPLES

ləɽke ki bəyhn.	The boy's sister.
ləɽkioŋ ki gwɽiaŋ.	The girl's dolls.
yuswf ke bhai ka ghoɽa.	The horse of Joseph's brother.
ghər ke dərvaze pər.	At the door of the house.

EXERCISE I

1. The boy's hand. 2. The man's ear. 3. The girl's hair (*pl.*). 4. The boy's tongue. 5. The hoof of the rider's horse. 6. The mother of the girls. 7. A hair of the horse's tail. 8. Women's work. 9. The man's movements. 10. In the boys' hands. 11. On tigers' heads. 12. Up to the doors of the houses.

LESSON II

ADJECTIVES; ADVERBS; COMPARISON

ADJECTIVES :—A qualifying adjective precedes its noun, and if liable to change agrees with it in gender and number, and also in form according to the table below. Most adjectives ending in a are liable to such change; those ending in any other sound are unchangeable. An adjective in the predicate agrees in gender and number with its noun in the subject : pynsyl choṭi həy, *the pencil is small.*

	Sing.		*Plural*	
	Masc.	*Fem.*	*Masc.*	*Fem.*
Nom.	bwra (*bad*)	bwri	bwre	bwri
Obl.	bwre	bwri	bwre	bwri

N.B.—The changes correspond exactly to those of ka, the sign of possession (see Lesson I).

COMPARISON :—There is no special form for comparative or superlative. When two objects are compared, that one with which the comparison is drawn is put in the oblique form with the postposition se, and the adjective conforms to the rule of the adjective : mera ghər twmhare ghər se uŋca həy, *my house is higher than your house*; twmhari pynsyl meri pynsyl se ləmbi həy, *your pencil is longer than mine.*

Sometimes zyada ; bəṛhkər, *more*, and əwr bhi, *still more*, are used as adverbs modifying the adjective : meri dival twmhari dival se zyada uŋci həy, *my wall is much higher than yours*; mwjh ko zyada batoŋ ki fwrsət nəhiŋ, *I have no leisure for further talk* (lit. *to me*, see p. 74); baɣ ki dival əwr bhi uŋci həy, *the garden wall is still higher.*

To express the superlative degree a universal comparison is made by using səb, *all*, with the postposition se : mera ghər səb se uŋca hai, *my house is the highest of all.*

Sometimes, when the thing referred to is not known to the speaker, the superlative is expressed by repeating the adjective and inserting the postposition se between : əcche se əccha mal lao, *bring the best stuff.*

ADVERBS :—Adjectives are often used as adverbs : **voh əccha bolta həy,** *he speaks well* ; **voh ghoɽa tez dəwɽa,** *that horse ran fast.*
" *Too* " is expressed by the simple adjective : **yeh dudh thoɽa həy,** *this milk is too little.* " *Very* " is expressed by **bəwht** : **yeh dudh bəwht gərm həy,** *this milk is very* (or *too*) *hot.*

N.B.—**Bəwht** with a singular noun means " *much*," with a plural " *many.*"

VOCABULARY

ka **qəyhva,** coffee	**bəɽa,** big
ki **pynsyl,** pencil	**miṭha,** sweet
ki **ca; cae,** tea	**cəwɽa,** wide
ki **cini ; ʃəkər,** sugar	**kəl,** yesterday ; to-morrow
tez, fast ; strong (tea)	**haŋ,** yes
choṭa, small (size)	**nəhiŋ,** no, not
taza, fresh	**lekyn ; məgər,** but

EXAMPLES

yeh dərya gənga (dərya) se choṭa həy.	This river is smaller than the Ganges.
twmhari zəmin ləmbi əwr cəwɽi həy.	Your ground is long and broad.
yeh hathi səb se bəɽa həy	This elephant is the largest of all.
twmhari pynsyl ki ləkɽi nərm həy ?	Is the wood of your pencil soft ?
nəhiŋ bəwht səxt həy.	No, it is very hard.
dudh zyada həy.	There is too much milk.
voh jəld se jəld dəwɽa ?	Did he run as quickly as possible ?

N.B.—The normal order of words in a sentence is : subject, object, and, last of all, the verb.

EXERCISE II

1. This is a swift horse ; it ran faster than yours yesterday.
2. This pencil is small, but that is still smaller. 3. Is this water fresh ? No, sir (**ji, nəhiŋ**), it is not fresh. 4. This is a big table ; it is very big ; it is the biggest in the house. 5. My tea is strong ;

it is too strong. 6. There is much sugar in my coffee ; it is too sweet. 7. Your table is long and wide ; it is bigger than mine ; it is very useful (bəwht kam ki).

LESSON III

PRONOUNS. ƏPNA

First Personal

	Singular		Plural
Nom.	məyŋ, *I*		həm, *we*
Obl.	mwjh, *me*		həm, *us*

N.B.—(1) The pronominal adjectives **mera**, *my, mine*, and **həmara**, *our, ours*, are used to denote possession.

(2) The direct and indirect object have alternate forms : **mwjh ko, mwjhe** ; **həm ko, həmeŋ**.

(3) Agent **ne** is attached to the nominative form in the singular : **məyŋ ne**.

(4) **həm**, with a plural verb, is sometimes used for *I*, and **həmara** for *my, mine*.

Second Personal

	Singular		Plural
Nom.	tu, *thou*		twm, *you*
Obl.	twjh, *thee*		,, ,,

N.B.—(1) The pronominal adjectives **tera**, *thy, thine*, and **twmhara**, *your, yours*, are used to denote possession.

(2) The direct and indirect object have alternate forms : **twjh ko, twjhe** ; **twmko, twmheŋ**.

(3) Agent **ne** is attached to the nominative form in the singular : **tu ne**.

(4) The singular forms are used in addressing the deity ; familiarly, as in the family circle ; and contemptuously ; consequently the forms **twm, twmhara** are used instead.

Third Personal

To express *he*, *she*, or *it*, the demonstrative pronouns **yeh**, *this*, and **voh**, *that*, are used.

ƏPNA :—(*a*) In sentences of the form *I . . . my . . .* ; *they . . . their . . .*, etc., where the pronominal adjective refers back to the subject akin in sense, then **əpna**, the possessive form of **ap**, *self* (see p. 71), must be used instead : **məyŋ . . . əpna . . .**, *I . . . my . . .*, etc. ; (*b*) **əpna** has also the sense of " *own* " : **mera əpna**, *my own* ; **ws ka əpna**, *his own* ; **əpna əpna**, *each his own* ; **əpne ap**, *of one's own accord* ; **əpne pas se**, *out of one's own " pocket."*

DEMONSTRATIVE, INTERROGATIVE, AND RELATIVE PRONOUNS

DEMONSTRATIVE		INTERROGATIVE	RELATIVE
Characteristic Sound **y**	**v** or **w**	**k**	**j**
Nom. **yeh**, *this* (*he, she, it*)	**voh**, *that* (*he, she, it*)	**kəwn**, *who* ?, *what* ? **kya**, *what* ?	**jo**, *who, which*
Obl. sing. **ys**	**ws**	**kys**	**jys**
Obl. pl. **yn**	**wn**	**kyn**	**jyn**

N.B.—(1) The oblique form for the direct and indirect object singular of **yeh** may be **ys ko** or **yse** ; and of the plural **yn ko** or **ynheŋ** ; the corresponding parts of **voh** may be **ws ko** or **wse** ; plural, **wn ko** or **wnheŋ**.

(2) **kəwn** is used with concrete nouns, **kya** with abstract. Both are used in indirect as well as direct questions : **voh kəwn həy**, *who is he* ? ; **məyŋ janta huŋ ky voh kəwn həy**, *I know who this is* (**ky** generally introduces a statement, see p. 39).

(3) **kya** is often used before an adjective in an exclamatory sense : **voh kya bevəquf həy**, *what a fool he is!* It is also frequently used without significance to introduce a question : **kya, yeh twmhari ʈopi həy**, *is this your hat* ?

(4) Interrogative particles are usually kept for emphasis close to the verb : **jo admi vəhaŋ həy voh kəwn həy**, *who is that man there* ?

A *

Indefinite Pronouns

Singular	*Singular*
Nom. koi (*someone, anyone*)	kwch (*some*)
Obl. kysi	

N.B.—(1) koi is followed by a verb in the singular; when used as a pronominal adjective, *any*, *some*, both noun and verb must be in the singular. The pronominal adjective kəi, *some*, *several*, serves as its plural.

(2) kwch as a pronoun is followed by a verb in the singular; as a pronominal adjective, *some*, it is sometimes used of persons also : kwch admi vəhaŋ həyŋ, *some persons are there.*

Vocabulary

ka bap, father
ki ghoɽi, mare
ki ciz, thing
ki kytab, book
ma bap (*m. pl.*), parents
əccha, good

bwra ; xərab, bad
myskin, quiet (animal)
ɣərib, poor
kala, black
əndha, blind
yəhaŋ, here

vəhaŋ, there
həy, is
həyŋ, are
tha (*m. s.*), was

Examples

mere ma bap yəhaŋ həyŋ lekyn ws ke yəhaŋ nəhiŋ (həyŋ).
: My parents are here, but his are not here.

jo log kəmre meŋ həyŋ voh səb buɽhe həyŋ.
: The people in the room are all old.

pitəl ki ek choṭi ḍybbi mez pər həy.
: A small brass casket is on the table.

yeh phəl kəcca həy lekyn voh am pəkke həyŋ.
: This fruit is unripe, but those mangoes are ripe.

N.B.—(1) The normal order of words in a sentence is : subject; object and adverbial expressions of time; place, and manner ; verb. Emphasis tends to bring important words towards the beginning. Negative and interrogative particles precede the verb closely.

(2) After **nəhiŋ** (=**na**, *not*, and **həyŋ**, *they are*) any part of the auxiliary present is often omitted.

(3) **səb**, *all*, when used as an adjective is not inflected ; when used as a noun it may take as oblique form **səbhoŋ**.

EXERCISE III

1. Here is a good man.   2. What a bad boy he was !   3. That mare is quiet ; she is blacker than my horse.   4. What is in your hand ?   It is my little daughter's doll.   5. Who is this person ? It is a poor woman.   6. What persons were at the door ?   They were blind men.   7. What is that in her hand ?   It is a small book.   8. They all were there yesterday.   9. This is my own book, not his.   10. That is his very own book.

LESSON IV

THE AUXILIARY VERB " HONA "

PART I

Hona, *to be*, *exist*, is its infinitive form.   All infinitives end in -na ; when this is removed the root or stem is left, from which several formations are obtained by additions to it : e.g. **ho**, **hota** (*pres. part.*), or **huŋga** (*fut. indic.*).

INDICATIVE

Present Tense

məyŋ huŋ, *I am*	**həm həyŋ**, *we are*
tu həy, *thou art*	**twm ho**, *you are*
voh həy, *he*, *she*, or *it is*	**voh həyŋ**, *they are*

N.B.—There is no distinction of genders in this tense.

Past Tense

məyŋ tha, or thi, *I was*	həm the, *we were*
tu tha, or thi, *thou wast*	twm the, or thiŋ, *you were*
voh tha, or thi, *he*, or *she was*	voh the, or thiŋ, *they were*

N.B.—thi, thiŋ are feminine singular and plural respectively. A distinction of genders is made in this and in all the remaining tenses except in 1st person plural, which has one form for both masculine and feminine, həm being always regarded as masculine save in the Panjab.

Future Tense : I shall, *or* will, be, etc.

məyŋ huŋga, or huŋgi	həm hoŋge
tu hoga, or hogi	twm hoge, or hogi
voh hoga, or hogi	voh hoŋge, or hoŋgi

N.B.—Other forms, e.g. hoega(i), hovega(i) in the singular, and hoveŋge(i) in the plural, are found.

Vocabulary

ka rəsta ; rasta, way
ka, ki dost, friend
ka, ki nəwkər, servant
log, people
jo, or jo koi, whoever
dusra, other, second

pwrana, ancient, old-time
mehnəti, diligent
kamyab, successful
xubsurət, beautiful
məzbut, strong
kəmzor, weak

jəvan, young
moţa, fat
dwbla, thin
ɣalybən, probably
zəra (*adv.*), just, a little

Examples

kytab kwtwb əlmari meŋ hogi.

twm kəl kəhaŋ the.

məyŋ ghər pər tha, mere səb ghər ke log vəhaŋ the.

twm kəl kəhaŋ hoge—yəhaŋ hoge ya dəftər (afys) meŋ ?

ws ki ţopi əlmari ke ek taq pər thi.

The book will be in the bookcase.

Where were you yesterday ?

I was at home ; all my family were there.

Where will you be to-morrow—here or in the office ?

His hat was on a shelf in the wardrobe.

Exercise IV

1. Who is that man ? He is my friend. 2. Who is the other person ? He is my old servant. 3. Whoever is diligent will probably be successful. 4. She will be a beautiful girl. 5. Is this your hat ? No, my hat is black. 6. Whose house is this ? It is my friend's (house) ; it is the highest in the street.

Substitution Table

voh	ləmba	mərd	bəwht	məzbut	həy
yeh	choţa	admi	zəra	kəmzor	tha
	jəvan	ləɽka	səb se	moţa	
	əndha			dwbla	

N.B.—Examples illustrating the use of the Table : **yeh jəvan admi bəwht dwbla həy; voh choţa ləɽka səb se məzbut tha.**

LESSON V

THE AUXILIARY VERB "HONA"

PART II. THE NEGATIVE

Subjunctive

Present : I may be *or* become, etc.

məyŋ huŋ	həm hoŋ
tu ho	twm ho
voh ho	voh hoŋ

N.B.—Uncontracted forms like **hoe, hove,** and **hoveŋ** occur.

Imperative

The imperative is identical in this verb with the present subjunctive as given above.

N.B.—The 2nd person singular and the root have the same form in all verbs ; the 2nd person plural adds **o**, but the contracted form **ho** is used in the case of this verb.

PARTICIPLES

The present participle consists of the root and -ta (roughly corresponding to the English -ing); and the past, of the root and -a (roughly corresponding to the English -ed, -en); in the particular case of this verb they are **hota** and **hua** respectively. Participial forms show the same changes for gender and number as adjectives ending in **a** (p. 6), except in the feminine plural when it is not followed by an auxiliary : e.g. hoti həyŋ, hwi thiŋ, but hotiŋ and huiŋ. There is a fuller form of the participles, with **hua** added : e.g. gyrta hua pətta, *a falling leaf*; gyre hue pətte, *fallen leaves* (from gyrna, *to fall*); hua in such instances emphasises the condition or state (see further, p. 51).

Tenses formed with present participle :

Habitual Present : məyŋ hota huŋ, etc., *I am being* or *becoming, I generally am,* etc.

This form makes a general statement of fact.

Habitual Past : məyŋ hota tha, etc., *I was becoming, I generally was,* etc.

This form likewise makes a general statement of fact.

For the use of the present participle in conditional and optional sentences, see p. 54.

Tenses formed with past participle :

Indicative :

Perfect : məyŋ hua, etc., *I was* or *became,* etc.

Pres. Perf.: məyŋ hwa huŋ, etc., *I have been* or *become,* etc.

Past Perf.: məyŋ hwa tha, etc., *I had been* or *become,* etc.

Fut. Perf.: məyŋ hwa huŋga, etc., *I will (must) have been* or *become,* etc.

Subjunctive :

Perfect : məyŋ hwa huŋ, etc., *I may have been* or *become,* etc.

For other uses of the participles, see p. 51.

N.B.—The root of **hona** combines with the present perfect and past perfect of **rəyhna,** *to remain,* to form a present tense : e.g. vəhaŋ kya ho rəha həy (tha), *what is (was) happening there now (then) ?* See further under rəyhna, p. 23.

NEGATIVES :

The negative particles are mət, na, and nəhiŋ (=na, *not*, and həyŋ, *they are*).

mət is prohibitive, and is used only with the imperative, or the infinitive used as a future or a semi-polite imperative.

na, or nə where unstressed, is used with any part except the present and present perfect of the indicative : **ho nə ho**, *whether or not, whether such be the case or not*.

nə frequently occurs as an enclitic after a verb, and expects a reply in the affirmative (cf. English and French usage) : **twm jaoge nə ?**, *you'll go, won't you ?*

nəhiŋ is used with any part except the subjunctive present and past, and is rare with the imperative or the infinitive used as an imperative (see p. 42), and if employed follows it : **bhulna nəhiŋ**, *don't forget*. After nəhiŋ (=nə +present auxiliary) the present auxiliary is often omitted as being tautological : **voh nəhiŋ gəe (həyŋ)**, *they have not gone*.

N.B.—ana, *to come* ; jana, *to go* (see p. 27).

" *Lest* " may be expressed in the following ways with the subjunctive :

mwjhe ḍər (xəwf) tha ky əysa nə ho ky voh na ae.	I feared lest he would not come.
mwjhe ḍər (xəwf) tha ky məyn vəqt pər na pəwhŋcuŋ.	I feared lest I would not arrive in time.
ws ka xəyal tha ky kəhiŋ cor na bhag jae.	He was apprehensive lest the thief should flee away.

" *If not, otherwise, or else* " is expressed by nəhiŋ to or vərna :

dəwṛo nəhiŋ to (vərna) twm vəqt pər nəhiŋ pəwhŋcoge.	Run or else you won't arrive in time.

The following distinctions require to be noted :

(*a*) həy, *is* (at the moment)
    malum həy (tha), *it is* (*was*) *known*
    malum hua, *it became known*

hota həy, *is*, *exists* (general statement of fact)
malum hota həy (tha), *it seems* (*seemed*)

(b) When " was " can be rendered by " became," it should be
translated by hua, or hogəya (past participle of ho-jana,
to become) : ws ko malum tha (hua), it was (became) known
to him.

VOCABULARY

ka janvər, animal

ka yəqin, certainty

ka saŋp, snake

ka mwlk, country, kingdom

ki bat, affair ; word, conversation

ki sərdi, cold

ki gərmi, heat

ap, sir, madam (a respectful
form requiring, when subject,
its verb in 3rd pers. pl.)

əhəmm, important, serious

mayus, despairing

xəbərdar, careful, cautious

səxt, severe ; hard

xwʃ, happy

ʃayəd, perhaps (*subjunct.*)

zərur, necessarily, certainly

kəbhi, ever

kəbhi kəbhi, sometimes

əb, əbhi, now

bhi, also, even

EXAMPLES

ghoṛa bəṛa janvər hota həy.

ys bat ka yəqin nəhiŋ (həy).

gaoŋ ke log əksər ɣərib hote
həyŋ.

ek janvər vəhaŋ zərur hoga.

voh əwrət əpne des ki dwʃmən
hogəi.

yəhaŋ ek hadysa hwa hoga.

pəyhle yəhaŋ bəwht bəṛe janvər
hote the.

ap ko mwbarəkbad ho, aj həm
səbhoŋ ke dyl meŋ xwʃi ho.

A horse (*collect.*) is a big animal.

This matter is not certain.

Villagers are generally poor.

There will (must) certainly be
an animal there.

That woman became an enemy
of her country.

There must have been an accident here.

Formerly many large animals
existed here.

Congratulations to you, Sir !
Let there be joy in the hearts
of all of us this day.

EXERCISE V

1. How big this horse is ! The horse is a big animal. 2. She
was here, but is not here now. 3. This is a difficult matter, but let
not anyone despair ! 4. Be careful, perhaps there may be a snake

there ! 5. In this country there is severe cold ; sometimes there is much heat. 6. Someone was certainly in this room ; someone must have been here. 7. Let none come into this room ; no one will go into that dark room. 8. Why have those villagers come here to-day ? 9. Believe it or not, it is true. 10. Perhaps the boy is here, and his mother also. 11. What's the matter ? There is nobody in the house ! 12. His parents are happy. May they be happy !

LESSON VI

FINITE VERB

PART I. INDICATIVE

bolna, *to make inarticulate sounds* (as the roaring of an animal) ; *to speak* (*to :* **ko** or **se**).

Habitual Present : məyŋ bolta (*fem.* bolti) huŋ, *I speak.*

məyŋ bolta (bolti) huŋ				həm bolte həyŋ			
tu	,,	,,	həy	twm	,,	(bolti) ho	
voh	,,	,,	həy	voh	,,	,,	həyŋ

Habitual Past : məyŋ bolta tha (*fem.* bolti thi), *I used to speak.*

məyŋ bolta tha (bolti thi)				həm bolte the			
tu	,,	,,	,,	,,	twm	,,	,,	(bolti thiŋ)
voh	,,	,,	,,	,,	voh	,,	,,	,,	,,

Present (continuous) : məyŋ bol rəha (rəhi) huŋ, *I am speaking.*

məyŋ bol rəha (rəhi) huŋ				həm bol rəhe həyŋ			
tu	,,	,,	,,	həy	twm	,,	,,	(rəhi) ho
voh	,,	,,	,,	,,	voh	,,	,,	,,	həyŋ

Imperfect (continuous) : məyŋ bol rəha tha (rəhi thi), etc., *I was speaking*, etc.

N.B.—Present and imperfect tenses are formed by adding the present perfect and past perfect respectively of **rəyhna** (*to remain*) to the root of any verb. **rəyhna** when added to other verbs has two significations ; it expresses the idea of (*a*) acting or proceeding at the moment, and (*b*) of continuity of action or proceeding. Both ideas, proceeding and continuing, are expressed by the present and imperfect tenses. The imperfect (continuous) refers to a definite time in the past : e.g. bəcpən meŋ voh təsvireŋ bəwht pəsənd kərta tha (habitual), *in childhood he was very fond of pictures*, but kəl təsvir voh ɣəwr se dekh rəha tha (continuous), *yesterday he was looking thoughtfully at the picture.*

Future : məyŋ boluŋga, etc., *I will or shall speak,* etc.

məyn boluŋga (boluŋgi)	həm boleŋge
tu bolega (bolegi)	twm bologe (bologi)
voh ,, ,,	voh boleŋge (boleŋgi)

Perfect :   məyŋ bola (boli), etc., *I spoke,* etc.
Present Perfect : məyŋ bola (boli) huŋ, etc., *I have spoken,* etc.
Past Perfect :   məyŋ bola tha (boli thi), etc., *I had spoken,* etc.
Future Perfect : məyŋ bola huŋga (boli huŋgi), etc., *I will have spoken,* etc.

VOCABULARY

ka gəvala, milkman
ka qwli, coolie
ka dhobi, washerman
ka kəpɽa, cloth
ka wstad, teacher
ka mahigir, fisherman
ka qyssa, story
ka jəhaz, ship
ka bavərci, cook
ka khana, food
ki gae, cow
ki aŋkh, eye
ki rel, train

ki rel-gaɽi, railway-carriage
sara, entire
saf, clean
əndhera, dark
kərna, to do
bat (bateŋ) kərna, to talk
sona, to sleep
swnna, to hear
(qyssa) kəyhna, to relate
   ,,   bəyan kərna, to relate
ladna, to load
pəkana, to cook

EXAMPLES

yeh kya ho rəha həy.

ws ke valydəyn stefən se a rəhe the.

ghoɽa ghas cərta həy.

ghoɽa ghas cər rəha həy.

What is this that is going on ?

His parents were coming from the station.

The horse (*collect.*) grazes.

The horse is grazing now.

ləɽkiaŋ khel ke məydan meŋ khel rəhi həyŋ.	The girls are playing in the sports-ground.
moci kys qysm ka kam kərta həy.	What kind of work does a cobbler do ?
voh cəmɽe se juti bənata həy.	He makes shoes of leather.
twm kya soc rəhe ho.	What are you thinking about ?
yeh qwli kya kam kər rəhe həyŋ.	What are these coolies doing ?
voh aʈe ki boriaŋ leja rəhe həyŋ.	They are carrying away sacks of grain.
ws ki aŋkhoŋ meŋ sari dwnya əndheri ho rəhi thi.	The whole world was going dark in her eyes.

EXERCISE VI

1. Where do the milkman's cows graze ? 2. Are his cows grazing there now ? 3. What sort of work do coolies do ? 4. Coolies do hard work. 5. The coolies were working hard. 6. This washerman does good work ; he makes the clothes clean ; he is washing clothes now. 7. We work by day and sleep by night. 8. The teacher is speaking ; when the teacher speaks the boys listen. 9. When the teacher was speaking, the boys were talking. 10. The fisherman was telling a story. 11. He was going to the bazaar ; his sister was not with him.* 12. The coolies are carrying sacks from the train ; they will load them on the ship. 13. What were you boys doing yesterday ? 14. The cook is cooking the food.

* ws ke sath—for " ke " expressions, see Lesson XXVII.

LESSON VII

FINITE VERB

PART II. SUBJUNCTIVE, ETC.

Present Subjunctive : məyŋ boluŋ, *I may speak.*

məyŋ boluŋ	həm boleŋ
tu bole	twm bolo
voh bole	voh boleŋ

Past Subjunctive : məyŋ bola (boli) huŋ, etc., *I may have spoken,* etc.

Imperative : məyŋ boluŋ, *let me speak.*

məyŋ boluŋ	həm boleŋ
tu bol	twm bolo
voh bole	voh boleŋ

N.B.—(*a*) The 2nd singular imperative is used in divine invocations, poetry, intimate and familiar relations such as the home-circle, and slightingly. Hence ordinarily it is replaced by

(*b*) 2nd plural imperative : yeh kam kəro, *do ye* or *you* (sing.) *this work.*

(*c*) A polite form is obtained by adding ie to the root : laie, *please bring* ; another by adding iega, which is also used as a polite future without any idea of command : boliega, *please speak* ; ap kəb jaiega, *when will you go, Sir ?* But in verbs whose roots end in e or i, jie and jiega respectively are added : pijie, *please drink* ; dijie, dijiega (for which the forms dije and dijega are sometimes used), *please give* ; ap kəb dijiega, *when will you give, Sir ?* ; ap bhul nə jaiega, *please don't forget, Sir* ; kərna, *to do, make,* is an exception : kijie, kijiega (for which kije, kijega are sometimes used).

(*d*) The infinitive is occasionally used as a semi-polite or a future imperative : yeh na kərna, *don't do this.*

(*e*) The 3rd plural subjunctive is considered the politest form of imperative : ap boleŋ, *please speak, Sir !*

Infinitive : bolna, *to speak.* For its various uses, see p. 41.

Participles : *Present*—bolta, bolta hua ; *Past*—bola, bola hua.

(*a*) Used as adjectives : ws ke mərte dəm tək, *until his dying breath* ; bhəra hua ghəɽa, *a full pitcher* ; məra hua admi, *a dead person.* See further, p. 52.

(*b*) For the use of the participles in conditional sentences, see p. 54.

(c) For the use of the participles in optative sentences, see p. 55.

(d) For the use of the participles to express state or condition, see p. 52.

Conjunctive Participle : Whereas English has a preference for short sentences, i.e. with finite verbs, connected by " and," Hindustani tends to reduce the number of finite verbs by including one or more of them in subordinate clauses. This is done in the clause by means of the conjunctive participle, i.e. through the particles **kǝr** or **ke** being added to the root of the verb in the clause : **voh xub sockǝr bola,** *having well pondered, he said* ; **voh kwrsi se wțhkǝr dǝrvaze ki tǝrǝf jakǝr ǝndhere meŋ ɣayb hogǝya,** *he rose up from the chair, and went to the door and disappeared in the darkness.* **kǝr** is the more common of the two particles ; the conjunctive participle of **kǝrna** is always **kǝrke** : **zǝra tǝklif kǝrke yeh kam kijie,** *please take a little trouble and do this task, be so good as to do this.*

The conjunctive participle expresses :

(a) priority in time, i.e. the action of its verb is previous to that of the finite verb ;

(b) manner : **hǝŋskǝr voh yeh bola,** *he said this laughingly* ;

(c) " although," i.e. it may have a concessive sense : **twm ytne bǝr̤e hokǝr chot̤e janvǝr se d̤ǝrte ho,** *though you are so big you are afraid of a small animal.*

N.B.—Concessive sentences are often introduced by **ǝgǝrcy,** *although,* and **bavwjudeky,** *although,* and the main clause, with the finite verb, by **lekyn,** or **mǝgǝr,** *but* ; **tǝw bhi,** or **phyr bhi,** *yet, still* : **ǝgǝrcy voh mǝzbut hǝy lekyn bǝhadwr nǝhiŋ,** *although he is strong, yet he is not brave* ; **bavwjudeky dǝrǝxt bǝwht bǝr̤a tha phyr bhi sidha nǝhiŋ tha,** *though tall the tree was not straight.*

The conjunctive participle may be repeated to express repetition of action : **kytabeŋ pǝr̤h pǝr̤hkǝr meri aŋkheŋ dwkhti hǝyŋ,** *from continually reading books my eyes give pain.*

For formations with **rǝyhna,** *to remain* or *stay,* see the following chapter.

VOCABULARY

ka nətija, result
ka ymtehan, examination
ka əxbar, newspaper
ka daṇt, tooth
ka ḍər, fear
ka surəj, sun
ka mil, mile
ka bazar, market
ka goʃt, flesh
ka sal, year
ki khyṛki, window
ki həva, wind

mwnasyb, proper, right
təiyar, ready
tez, sharp
ṭhənḍa, cold
dur, distant
phyr, again
vapəs, back
ləwṭna, to return
kaṭna, to bite, cut
wṭhna, to rise
nykəlna, to come out
pina, to drink

EXAMPLES

ʃayəd voh aj ae (aega).

Perhaps he (she) will come to-day.

ho nə ho məyŋ xwʃ huŋga.

Whether or not, I shall be happy.

xwda jane kya hoga.

God knows what will happen !

koi jane nə jane məyŋ nəhiŋ janta.

Someone may know, but I don't.

wn meŋ se ʃayəd hi koi jita bəca.

Hardly anyone among them was saved alive.

ʃayəd hi ytni kamyabi kysi ko nəsib hwi ho.

Seldom will such success have fallen to anyone's lot.

məyŋ cahta huŋ ky təmam ʃəyhr dekhuŋ.

I wish to see the whole city.

caho nə caho əysa hi hoga.

Whether you desire it or not, it shall be !

əngṛai lekər voh kwrsi se wṭha.

He yawned and got up from the chair.

mere lie qəyhva lakər ghər jao.

Bring me coffee and then go home.

məyŋ əbhi khakər aya huŋ.

I ate just before coming.

əgərcy voh mwskərata həy təw bhi ɣwsse həy.

Though he is smiling yet he is angry.

voh məkan yəhaŋ se car mil dur (or, car mil ke fasle pər) həy.

That building is four miles distant from here.

tin həfte hue ky voh lahəwr   Three weeks have passed since
pəwhŋca.   he arrived in Lahore.

EXERCISE VII

1. It is right that you should go. 2. Am I to go ? No, stay
here. 3. He went away, but perhaps he will come again.
4. The result of the examination is ready ; perhaps you will
read it in to-morrow's newspaper. 5. Sit; please sit here; will
you please sit on this chair, Sir ! 6. Take care ! That animal
may bite you ; its teeth are very sharp. 7. He rose from the
chair and went towards the window. 8. Big as he was, he was
afraid and ran away. 9. Though the sun had come out, yet the
wind was cold. 10. His house is the highest in the street ; it is
two miles distant from the market. 11. Dogs eat flesh ; cats
drink milk. 12. The cat will drink and go outside, but the dog
will eat and remain indoors. 13. It is a week since he arrived
here. 14. Does this river flow all the year through?

LESSON VIII

RƏYHNA

rəyhna by itself means " *to remain, stay* " : cwp rəho, *keep quiet* ;
voh kəhaŋ rəyhte həyŋ, *where do they live ?* ; voh bahər rəhi, *she
remained outside.*

In combination with another verb it has two uses, expressing
(*a*) action or procedure at the moment, and (*b*) continuity.

(*a*) At p. 17 its present perfect and past perfect have been
shown added to the root of another verb to form the present
(continuous) and imperfect (continuous) tenses respectively of
the latter :

Present (Cont.) Tense : voh kya kər rəha həy, *what is he doing ?*
  (root + *Pres. Perf.*) voh cyṭṭhi lykh rəha həy, *he is writing a
                            letter.*
                          həm swn rəhe həyŋ, *we are listening.*
                          voh sṭeʃən se a rəhe həyŋ, *they are coming
                            from the station.*

Imperf. (*Cont.*) *Tense:*　əwrət kya kər rəhi thi,　*what was the*
(root + *Past Perf.*)　　　　*woman doing ?*

　　　　　　　　　　voh ca pi rəhi thi, *she was drinking tea.*
　　　　　　　　　　voh bol nəhiŋ rəhi thiŋ, *they* (f.) *were not*
　　　　　　　　　　　　speaking.

N.B.—See p. 29 for another phrasal construction (with **kərna**) to express this habitual or frequentative sense more emphatically.

(b) (1) The forms and examples in (a) also express continuity :

voh stʃeʃən se a rəhe həyŋ.	*They are coming along from the station.*
ws ki ʃwhrət pwrane zəmane se cəli a rəhi həy (see p. 59.)	*Its fame has endured from ancient time.*

(2) Continuity is also expressed by the perfect tense of **rəyhna** added to the present participle of the main verb :

voh swnte rəhe.	*They kept on listening.*
əwrət roti rəhi.	*The woman went on weeping.*
voh syskiaŋ leti rəhi.	*She kept on sobbing.*

Also by the future of **rəyhna** :

ghoɽa bəwht der tək dəwɽta rəhega.	*The horse will keep on running for a long time.*

(3) A stronger sense of continuity is conveyed by employing the habitual tenses with the present participle of the main verb :

voh khate rəyhte həyŋ.	*They keep on eating.*
voh bateŋ kərti rəyhti thiŋ.	*They were going on and on talking.*

The following uses of **rəyhna** are of a different nature :

1. Its root combines with **jana** to form a compound having the meaning " *to remain over, be left behind* " :

syrf paŋc rwpəe rəyh gəe.	*Only five rupees remained.*
bəwht saman rəyh gəya.	*Much luggage was left behind.*

2. The form jata rəha signifies " *to be completely lost*," and is only used idiomatically :

ws ka bazu ləɽai meŋ jata rəha.	*His arm was lost in battle.*
jəb kəlam məŋ təkəllwf pəyda hojata həy to sadəgi hath se jati rəyhti həy.	*When formalism is introduced into speech simplicity is lost.*

3. The intransitive verb **sona** (*to sleep*) when combined with **rəyhna** has a sense of " *going to sleep intentionally* " : **voh so rəha**, *he* (*deliberately*) *went to sleep* ; but not so when combined with **jana** : **voh so gəya**, *he fell asleep.*

VOCABULARY

ka ghənʈa, hour ; gong ; bell	*ki* niŋd, sleep
ka ʃor, noise	*ki* fəwj, army
ka moɽ, corner, bend	*ki* ʃam, evening
ka pəyhra, guard	gəyhra, deep
ka axyr, end	khəɽa, erect, standing
ka cavəl, rice	təndrwst, healthy
ka gyrja, church	bəhadwr, brave
ka gəɽha, hole	təmam, entire
ka bədən, body	həmeʃa, always
ka rysala, cavalry	apəs meŋ, together, mutually
ki pyada pəlʈən, infantry	maŋgna, to ask for, want
ki bhik, alms	khodna, to dig

EXAMPLES

məyŋ swn rəha tha.	I was listening.
voh nəhiŋ swn rəha tha.	He was not listening.
voh so rəha həy.	He is asleep.
voh bəwht der tək soya rəha.	He slept till late.
voh sone ke lie ja rəha həy.	He is going off to bed.
ek ghənʈa hua voh sone ko gəya.	He went off to bed an hour ago.
voh gəyhri niŋd sota həy.	He sleeps soundly.
voh gəyhri niŋd so rəha həy.	He is sleeping soundly.
ʃor ke bavwjud voh soe rəha.	He slept on notwithstanding the noise.
badəl bəwht gərəj rəha həy.	There is a great deal of thunder.

byjli cəməkti rəyhti həy.	The lightning keeps on flashing.
həmare sypahi dwʃmən ke mwqabələ meŋ səxt ləɽai ləɽ rəhe the.	Our soldiers were fighting hard against the enemy.
raste ke moɽ pər ek bhik maŋgne valà so rəha həy.	At the bend of the road a beggar is asleep.
voh həmeʃa pəyhre pər so jata həy.	He always goes to sleep on duty.
voh jəb kəbhi pəyhre pər jata həy so jata həy.	Whenever he goes on duty he falls asleep.
voh jəhaŋ kəhiŋ pəyhre pər gəya so gəya.	Wherever he went on duty he fell asleep.
jo kwch rəyh gəya voh bad meŋ laya.	Whatever was left behind he brought afterwards.
voh raste ke axyr tək bəhadwri se cəlte rəheŋge.	They will keep on bravely till the end of the road.
həm apəs meŋ ydhər wdhər ki bateŋ kər rəhe the.	We were conversing about nothing in particular among ourselves.

Exercise VIII

1. She is standing ; she remained standing ; she will remain here. 2. He eats rice ; he is not eating ; he keeps on eating ; he kept on eating. 3. The padre is going to the church ; he goes to the church ; he is coming along to the church. 4. He is digging a deep hole ; the labourers were digging a deep hole ; they were digging deep holes here and there. 5. What are you doing ? What were you doing yesterday ? What will you be doing to-morrow ? 6. She runs well (əcchi) ; she keeps on running ; she kept running on and on. 7. There was a man going along ; with him was a little dog. 8. With exercise the body remains healthy. 9. The brave man fears no one. 10. An army is approaching ; in it are cavalry and infantry. 11. He remained on guard the entire night. 12. That child is crying ; why is he crying ? he is always crying ; he cries day and night ; he pouts his lips and cries. 13. He goes to office daily ; he comes from office in the evening ; he is coming now ; he keeps coming along.

LESSON IX

IRREGULARITIES IN VERBS

THE verb in Hindustani is extremely regular; the only irregularities, besides those in the auxiliary hona, *to be* (see p. 11), are
represented in the following list :

| VERB | PARTICIPLES | | IMPERATIVE | | |
	Pres.	Past	2nd Sing.	2nd Pl.	Polite Form
ana, *to come*	ata	aya	a	ao	aie
jana, *to go*	jata	gəya	ja	jao	jaie
lana, *to bring*	lata	laya	la	lao	laie
lena, *to take*	leta	lia	le	lo	lijie
dena, *to give*	deta	dia	de	do	dijie; dije
pina, *to drink*	pita	pia	pi	pio	pijie
kərna, *to do*	kərta	kia	kər	kəro	kijie, kije

N.B.—(*a*) Verbs whose roots end in a add ya, and those in e
change this to i, before the final a of the past participle : aya; dia.

(*b*) The regular past participle of jana, viz. jaya, is used with
kərna when the latter means " *to be in the habit of* " (see p. 29) :
voh vəhaŋ jaya kərta tha, *he was in the habit of going there.*

kəra, the regular past participle of kərna, is occasionally used
in Hindi.

(*c*) The feminine and inflected masculine forms of the following
are :

	Fem.	Infl.
aya	ai	ae
gəya	gəi	gəe
laya	lai	lae

(*d*) The above verbs, with the exception of pina, occur in a
great variety of expressions; some of the more common are
indicated in the following examples :

ana :

twm ko ys bat pər ʃərm nəhiŋ
ati.
*Are you not ashamed of this
affair ?*

kəl ws ko bwxar aya lekyn aj
voh əccha həy.
*Yesterday he had fever, but to-day
he is well.*

wse mwjh pər həsəd aya.	*He was envious of me.*
səb phəloŋ meŋ se am mwjhe zyada (bəɽhkər) pəsənd həy (ata həy).	*Of all fruits I like the mango best.*
mwjhe hyndostani nəhiŋ ati.	*I cannot speak Hindustani.*
ek wmda ciz mere hath ai.	*I got a splendid article.*
yeh ciz ws ke kam aegi.	*This thing will be useful to him.*
yeh jutiaŋ paoŋ meŋ ʈhik nəhiŋ atiŋ.	*These shoes don't fit well.*
ek pəhaɽ əcanək (yəkayək) nezər aya.	*A mountain suddenly appeared.*
ws ki nəzər ys saedar dərəxt pər pəɽi.	*His eye fell on this shady tree.*
voh aŋkhoŋ pər cəʃma dwrwst kərke təsvir ki tərəf nəzər uʈhane ləga.	*He adjusted his spectacles and began to raise his glance towards the picture.*
əyse xubsurət əwr dylcəsp mənzər pər nəzər ɖalne se dyl xwʃ hojata həy.	*From casting a glance on such a beautiful and charming scene the heart becomes glad.*

jana :

ws ki bat pər mat jao.	*Don't take his word for it.*
ws ke phəʈe pwrane kəpɽoŋ pər na jaie.	*Don't be taken in (judge) by his torn old clothes.*

lana :

lana is probably composed of **lena** and **ana**. **leana**, *to fetch*, and **lejana**, *to take away*, are in common use.

ɣərib log rəddi bhi kam meŋ late həyŋ.	*Poor people make use even of waste.*
voh ws məzhəb pər iman laya.	*He became a convert to (put faith in) that religion.*
voh yslam laya.	*He accepted Islam (became a Muslim).*

lena :

baz log rəddi (kaɣəz) se bhi kam lete həyŋ.	*Some people use even waste (paper).*
voh dəs rwpəe qərz lena cahta həy.	*He wishes to take a loan of ten rupees.*
jhil ləyhreŋ leti (khati) həy.	*There are ripples on the lake.*

voh əngɽai (ḍəkar) lekər bola.   *He said with a yawn (belch).*

bənia len den meŋ məsruf rəyhta həy.   *The shopkeeper is occupied with business.*

əwrət hyckiaŋ le rəhi thi.   *The woman was hiccuping.*

dena :

jane do.   *Let it go (pass) !*

ek nehayət wmda məyhəl dykhai dia.   *An extremely fine palace appeared.*

For **dena, dylana,** see further, p. 37.

kərna :

voh vəhaŋ jane se ynkar kərega.   *He will refuse to go (deny going) there.*

zəra təklif kərke pynsyl dije.   *Be so good as to (taking a little trouble) give me a pencil.*

mehrbani kərke pynsyl dijie   *Be so kind as to give me a pencil.*

ys ṭuṭe bəks ki mərəmmət kəro (kərao).   *Repair (get repaired) this broken box.*

mera moza rəfu kəro.   *Darn my sock (stocking).*

voh mwjh pər əysi bəɽi ynayət kərega.   *He will do me such a great favour.*

voh mwjh pər ytna bəɽa ehsan kərega.   *He will show me such great kindness.*

voh rwpia (qərz) əda kərega.   *He will pay the money (debt).*

kərna, *to do,* or *make,* when added to the masculine singular past participle of another verb is intransitive and means " *to be in the habit of* " (see *N.B.* (*b*) above) :

voh roz swbəh səvere wṭha kərta tha.   *He was in the habit of getting up early every day.*

voh hər roz kwch pəɽha kərti thi.   *She used to read something daily.*

voh həmeʃa ʃagyrdoŋ ko yeh takid kia kərta tha.   *He always used to enjoin this on the pupils.*

When the past tense of **kərna** occurs in this construction it may indicate either continued or habitual action : **həm vəhaŋ**

rəha kie, *we were in the habit of,* or *continued, staying there* ;
yeh bat həmeʃa hua ki, *this always used,* or *continued, to
happen.*

A "*habit*" is rendered by adət, the adjective of which is adi,
accustomed, addicted : ws ko məydan meŋ həva khane ki adət həy,
he is in the habit of going for an airing in the park ; voh əfim khane
ka adi həy, *he is addicted to opium-eating.*

The direct form of transmitting a statement is generally used,
i.e. the actual words of the speaker are repeated.

(*a*) With the finite tenses of verbs meaning "*to say, think, wish,
feel,*" etc., direct narration is general :

məyŋ dəftəri ko kəhuŋga ky lebəl bəks pər (se) səreʃ (goŋd) se ləgao.	*I'll order the daftari to stick the label on with glue (gum).*

(*b*) After the imperative of a verb denoting "*to order,*" bolna,
kəyhna, hwkm dena, indirect narration with ky and the subjunctive is general :

byjli mystri ko kəho ky ḍhile tar joɽe.	*Order the electrician to join up the loose wires.*

nəwkər ko (se) kəho ky yəhaŋ ae.
  ,,   ,,   ,, bolo ,,   ,,   ,,
  ,,   ,,   ,, yəhaŋ ane ko kəho.
  ,,   ,, yəhaŋ ane ka hwkm do.
  ,,   ,, hwkm do ky yəhaŋ ae.

      Order the servant to come here.

VOCABULARY

ka əndhera, darkness
ki mwafi, forgiveness
ki pəgɽi, pagri (turban)
ki mom bətti, wax-candle
ki byjli bətti, electric light
ki məchli, fish
ki fəjr, dawn
ki der, delay
bənd, closed
sidha, straight
dayaŋ (*infl.* daeŋ), right
bayaŋ (*infl.* baeŋ), left

həṭna, to go backwards
jəlana, to light, kindle
bwjhana, to extinguish
ghumna (*intr.*), to turn round
ghwmana (*tr.*), to turn round
khwlna, to be open.
kholna, to open
wbəlna (*intr.*), to boil
wbalna (*tr.*), to boil
bwlana, to call, summon
bwlvana, to cause to be sum-
    moned.

EXAMPLES

twm kəhaŋ se ae ho.	Where have you come from ?
tum kəl kəhaŋ gəe.	Where did you go yesterday ?
məyŋ ws ke sath jauŋga.	I shall go with him.
məyn ws ka sath duŋga.	I shall accompany him.
roṭi dudh mere vaste (*or* lie) lao.	Bring me bread and milk.
chwri kaŋṭa mwjhe do.	Give me a knife and fork.
yeh lejao əwr dusra lao.	Take this away and bring another.
voh hər roz ʃəyhr (ko) jati həy.	She goes to town every day.
pərda wṭhao ta ky dhup bhitər ae.	Raise the curtain so that daylight may enter.
pərda ḍalo əwr ləymp jəlao.	Draw the curtain and light the lamp.
sais ko hwkm do ky ghoṛa yəhaŋ jəldi lae.	Order the groom to bring the horse here quickly.
jəldi (se) təiyari kije.	Make preparation quickly.
sais ko kəyh do (kəho) ky kale ṭəṭṭu ko cəkkər de.	Order the syce to lunge the black pony.
ws se kəho ky fəwrən jae.	Order him to go at once.
mere lie ṭəyksi məngvaie— məyŋ sṭeʃən jane ko huŋ.	Order (send for) a taxi for me ; I am going to the station.
mwjhe kwch ʃorba cahie ; xydmətgar ko kəho ky ʃorba lae (ʃorba lane ke lie kəho).	I want some soup ; tell the waiter (table-servant) to bring the soup.

N.B.—(1) əwr (*and*) is usually omitted between two nouns commonly associated (e.g. chwri kaŋṭa).

(2) se is often omitted after jəldi.

EXERCISE IX

1. Come here ; come over here ; come quick ; come slowly.
2. Who goes there ? Please go away ; go over there. Back, back ! 3. Take this book. Will you take this book ? I will not take it. 4. Please forgive me—I will do my task. 5. Bring me the black hat ; fetch his white pagri. 6. Speak, speak ! What shall I speak ? Tell her this. 7. It is dark in this room ; light the candle—or rather, switch on the light. Switch off that light.
8. Go straight ahead ; turn to the right hand ; turn left ; turn round ; turn the carriage round. 9. Open the door ; close the

window. 10. Bearer, tell the cook to come here. Sir, the cook is not in the house ; he went to the market, but will come soon (thoṛi der bad). 11. Sir, there are three fish-dishes to-day. Very good, I would like boiled fish, but give the order now so that there may not be delay. 12. Call a servant ; please call a carriage ; send for a carriage. 13. He is in the habit of writing something every day. 14. I am accustomed to wake at dawn every day and to rise early. 15. He is wont to dine daily at noon. 16. I made it a practice to read three hours every morning.

LESSON X

DIRECT OBJECT. AGENT—NE

THE postposition **ko** (when it is not the sign of the indirect object, or used in an adverbial phrase, e.g. **dyn ko**, *by day*) is usually the sign of a definite direct object.

chwri lao will usually mean " *bring a knife*," but may mean " *bring the knife*," as the object is inanimate. (See *N.B. (a)* below.)

chwri ko lao will usually mean " *bring the knife*," but **ko** is sometimes added to an indefinite or an inanimate object to avoid ambiguity as to which word is subject and which object. (See *N.B. (b)* below.)

N.B.—(a) When the direct object is a person, a proper name, an interrogative or a personal pronoun, being definite it is put in the inflected form with **ko**. This rule is occasionally not observed with persons ; occasionally it is observed with inanimate objects to particularise them.

(b) An indefinite direct object may be put in the inflected form with **ko** to avoid ambiguity : **hira ʃiʃe ko kaṭṭa həy**, *a diamond cuts glass*.

(c) The demonstrative pronouns and adjectives (**yeh**, **voh**), being in themselves definite, may be either inflected or uninflected : **yeh cəmca** or **ys cəmce ko saf kəro**, *clean this spoon*.

An adjective, whether preceding its noun or in the predicate, agrees with it in gender, number, and form, but if the noun be the direct object with ko, the adjective in the predicate must be masculine singular and uninflected : gaɽi dərwaze pər khəɽi kəro, but gaɽi ko dərvaze pər khəɽa kəro, *make the carriage stand at the door*.

Agent ne.   When the Hindustani verb in a sentence is transitive, i.e. takes a direct object and is in one of the past tenses (including the perfect subjunctive), the subject is put in the oblique form with ne, the agent-sign, which marks the subject as the source of the action affecting the direct object; the verb is then made to agree in gender and number with the direct object : ws ne cyṭṭhi lykhi, *he wrote a letter*; bəndər ne ws ka hath kaṭa, *a monkey bit his hand*.   This construction is based according to one theory on an old passive form, differing from the modern passive form (see p. 56), and the former sentence might be rendered literally : *by him a letter written*, or impersonally : *by him a letter there was written*.

But if the direct object is accompanied by ko, then the verb must take the form of the masculine singular of the past participle: ws ne ys cyṭṭhi ko lykha həy, *he has written this letter* ; twm ne əysə barik zevər ko dekha həy? *have you ever seen such a dainty ornament?*

This construction with ne is necessary even if the direct object is not expressed :   kya, twm ne dekha, *did you see?*

N.B.—(*a*) The following verbs though transitive are exceptions to this rule of ne : bəkna, *to speak foolishly* ; bolna (rarely with ne), *to speak* ; bhulna, *to forget* ; lana, *to bring*.   In the case of səməjhna, *to understand*, ne is optional, but rare : ap meri bat səmjhe? *did you understand what I said?* ; məyŋ (ne) ys bat ko nəhiŋ səmjha, *I did not understand this matter*.

jitna, *to win*, and harna, *to lose*, when used with bazi, *game*, ʃərt, *bet*, may or may not take ne, but do not take ne when there is no object.

(*b*) The first and second personal pronouns retain before ne their nominative forms : e.g. məyŋ ne ; twm ne.

The following forms before ne are also to be noted : ynhoŋ, wnhoŋ, *they* ; jynhoŋ, *who, which* ; kynhoŋ? *who? which?* But when these pronouns become pronominal adjectives then the forms yn, wn, jyn, kyn, must be used : wnhoŋ ne təmaʃa

B

dekha, *they saw the show*, but wn becare beccoŋ ne təmaʃa nəhiŋ dekha, *those unlucky children did not see the show*.

After the direct object in the form mwjhe, həmeŋ ; twjhe, tumheŋ ; yse, ynheŋ ; wse, wnheŋ, the rule of ko must be used, i.e. the verb must take the form of the masculine singular of the past participle.

VOCABULARY

ka pyar, affection
ka wllu, owl
ka səfha, page (book)
ka ʃykari, hunter
ka əjayb xana, museum (lit. house of wonders)
ki cil, kite
ki cuhi, mouse

ki dəvat, inkstand
ki chwʈʈi, leave of absence
bhukha, hungry
pyasa, thirsty
əjib, wonderful
məngana, to send for
məngvana, to send for

EXAMPLES

yse ws ko do.	Give this to him.
ek chwri kaŋʈa mez pər rəkho.	Lay a knife and fork on the table.
mere lie chwriaŋ kaŋʈe əwr cəmce lao.	Bring me knives, forks and spoons.
swkh dwkh choʈe bəroŋ ke nəsib meŋ hota həy.	Joy and sorrow are the lot of big and small.
lərke lərkiaŋ ek sath khel rəhe the.	The boys and girls were playing together.
voh lərke əwr lərkioŋ se bola əwr (ws ne) wn ko (wnheŋ) kwch dia.	He spoke to the boys and the girls, and gave them something.
koi həmare caŋdi ke bərtən ko legəya hoga.	Someone must (will) have removed our silver dish.
ws ne sygrəʈ dan (cae dan) mez pər rəkha.	She put the cigarette-box (teapot) on the table.
nəwkər ne ca (cae) bənai thi.	The servant had made the tea.
lərki ne khyrki se awaz di.	The girl called out from the window.
twm ne meri sui ko kya kia.	What did you do with my needle ?
ws ne əpne pwrane jute ko kya kia.	What did he do with his old shoes ?

ws ne bwnne ka hwnər sikha.

ws ne zəxmi cyɽia ko əpne nərm nazwk hath se wʈhaya.

He learned the art of weaving.

She lifted the wounded little bird with her soft, delicate hand.

meri səməjh meɳ nəhiɳ ata həy ky twm kya bək rəhe ho (twm kya bəkvas kər rəhe ho).

I don't understand this utter nonsense of yours.

N.B.—(*a*) **ko** marking the direct object and **ko** the indirect in the same short sentence should be avoided.

(*b*) The omission of **əwr** (*and*) between two nouns habitually associated is frequent : **roʈi məkkhən do**, *give bread and butter.*

Exercise X

1. Give me a book ; please give me the book ; be so good as to give this book to your son. 2. The mother loves the daughter, and the daughter her mother. 3. A kite preys on (**ka ʃykar kərna**) small animals ; the owl is hunting mice ; the cat will eat the mouse. 4. Call a servant ; summon the bearer ; I'll call my servant. 5. Order the bearer to place a pen and inkstand on the table ; someone must have placed this inkstand on the table. 6. There was only a little bread in the house ; the mistress (**memsahb**) sent for some more. 7. The women were hungry and thirsty ; they ate the bread and drank the milk ; they drank much cold water. 8. He called all the servants into the house. 9. She asked for one day's leave. 10. I have read a few pages of this book. 11. Did you write the letter to your friend yesterday ? 12. What wonderful things did you see in the museum yesterday ?

LESSON XI

LƏGNA; DENA; PANA

ləgna, when it means " *to begin,*" **dena**, " *to allow,*" and **pana**, " *to manage to, to be allowed,*" take the accompanying verb in the inflected form of the infinitive ; **ləgna** and **pana** do not admit of the agent **ne** construction.

ləgna is an intransitive verb meaning " *to attach itself to*," and then " *to begin*." With the latter meaning it presents no difficulty of construction :

voh kam kərne ləga.	*He began to work.*
rel chwʈne ləgi.	*The train began to move off.*
ws ka dymaɣ cəkrane ləga.	*His brain began to be in a whirl.*

Its primary significance, however, admits of a number of constructions with the postpositions ko (often of the person) : meŋ, *in* ; pər, *on* ; se, (*adhering*) *to* :

mwjh ko bhukh (pyas) ləgi. məyŋ bhukha (pyasa) huŋ.	*I am hungry (thirsty).*
ws ko sərdi ləgi.	*He caught a chill.*
ws ka pəta mwjh ko (mwjhe) nəhiŋ ləga.	*I found no trace of him (it).*
ws ko, or ws ke (bədən meŋ), səxt coʈ ləgi.	*He got a severe wound.*
yeh bat ws ko bwri ləgi.	*He took this matter to heart (took it badly).*
əysi pəgʈi ws ko əcchi nəhiŋ ləgti.	*This kind of pagri does not suit him.*
əysi nəfis ciz twm ko kəhaŋ se hath ləgi.	*Where did you obtain such an exquisite thing ?*
sone ke kəmre meŋ ag ləgi.	*The bedroom caught fire.*
ghoʈa gaʈi meŋ ləga (jwta) hwa həy.	*The horse has been yoked.*
ys kam pər kəm se kəm pəcas məzdur ləge həyŋ.	*At least fifty labourers are working on this job.*
voh əpne kam meŋ ləgi rəyhti həy.	*She is intent on her own work.*
vəhaŋ jane meŋ kytne dyn ləgeŋge.	*How many days will it take to go there ?*
twmhare ane meŋ bəwht der ləgi.	*You have come late.*
ws ləmbe səfər meŋ do həzar rwpia ləga.	*Two thousand rupees were expended on that long journey.*
dekho ky cabi tale (qwfl) meŋ ləgti həy.	*See if the key fits the padlock (lock).*
ws ke nam pər dhəbba ləga.	*There is a stain on his good name.*
ys dwkan pər kytna xərc ləga.	*How much was the expenditure upon this shop ?*

dərəxt pər pəkke am ləgte həyŋ.   *There are ripe mangoes on the tree.*

ws ki zəban talu se ləgi.   *His tongue cleaved to his palate.*

ghər ghər se ləga həy.   *House touches house.*

The transitive of ləgna is ləgana :

ws ka pəta ləgao.	*Find out where he (it) is.*
phyr der mət ləgao.	*Don't be late again.*
xub zor ləgao.	*Apply your strength.*
wnhoŋ ne ʃəyhr ke jənub meŋ bayat ləgae.	*They laid out gardens (orchards) south of the town.*
pətlun meŋ pəyvənd ləgao.	*Put a patch in the trousers.*
ys təxte meŋ ek ləmbi kil ləgao.	*Drive a long nail into this board.*
ys kam pər səw məzdur ləgao.	*Put a hundred workmen on this job.*
bəks pər rəng ləgao.	*Paint the box.*
dəva ws ke hath pər ləgao.	*Put medicine on his hand.*
yeh tar ws dəndi se ləgao.	*Attach this wire to that rod.*
dyl (ji) ləgakər pərho.	*Study diligently.*
maŋ ne bete ko gəle ləgake rwxsət kia.	*The mother embraced her son and bade him farewell (sent him off).*

dena, *to give, allow.* When it has the former meaning it may take a direct and an indirect object, and its past tenses require agent ne with the subject :

pəwdoŋ ko pani do.	*Water the plants.*
voh səxi həy, həmeʃa yəriboŋ ko mədəd deta həy.	*He is generous, he always gives help to the poor.*
wnhoŋ ne car car rwpəe die.	*They gave four rupees each.*
ws ne mwsafyr ka sath dia.	*He accompanied the traveller.*

When it signifies " *to allow* " it takes the inflected infinitive of the other verb, and its past tenses require agent ne with the subject :

jane do.	*Let it go (don't bother about it)!*
mwjhe age bərhne dije.	*Please let me proceed forward.*
ws ne mwjhe cəlne na (nəhiŋ) dia.	*He did not let me proceed.*
dərban ne wn ko ehate meŋ jane na dia.	*The doorkeeper did not let them enter the compound.*

yjazət (*permission*) **hona**, or **dena**, is often used in such sentences :

mwjhe bhitər ane ki yjazət həy ?	*May I come in ?*
dərban ne yjazət na di.	*The gatekeeper did not give permission.*
əpne baɣ meŋ zəra səyr kərne ki yjazət dijiega ?	*Will you permit me to walk a little in your garden ?*

The causal form of **dena** is **dylana**, *to cause* (*something*) *to be given* (*by someone*) :

məyŋ ne wse ws berəyhm admi se paŋc rwpəe dylae.	*I made that cruel person give him five rupees.*

It is also used with the meaning " *to give* " :

sərdar ne wn ke ji meŋ wmed (wmmed) dylai.	*The leader inspired hope in their mind.*
məyŋ ne ws ko yəqin dylaya.	*I gave him assurance.*
ws ne roti hui maŋ ko təsəlli dylai.	*He consoled the weeping mother.*
voh do lərkiaŋ ek dusre ko maŋ ke vade ki yad dylati thiŋ.	*The two girls reminded each other of their mother's promise.*

dena is intransitive in the following constructions :

pəhaɽ dur se saf (xub) dykhai dete həyŋ.	*Mountains are clearly visible from afar.*
hər jəgəh swnsan thi, koi avaz swnai nəhiŋ deti thi.	*Every place was desolate ; not a sound could be heard.*
ghoɽa pəkɽai na dia.	*The horse would not be caught.*
yəkayək bəmbaroŋ ka dəsta dykhai dia.	*Suddenly a bomber-squad came in sight.*
əcanək golabari ki avaz swnai di.	*Suddenly the sound of shell-fire was heard.*

It is intransitive in this compound with **cəlna** :

cor dər ke mare cəl die (see p. 60).	*The thieves cleared off through fear.*

pana, *to obtain, find, be allowed, manage to*. When it means " *to* *obtain or find* " a sense of search or effort is involved, in distinction from **mylna**, *to get by chance* (see p. 75).

məyŋ ne əpni khoi hui cabi pai.	*I found my lost key.*
dwʃmən ne ʃəyhr pər qabu na paya.	*The enemy obtained no hold on the city.*
jəyse kəroge vəyse paoge.	*As you act so will you get.*
ws ne jəysa kia vəysa hi paya.	*As he acted just so did he receive.*
ws ne ymtehan məŋ pəyhla nəmbər hasyl kia əwr əccha ynam paya.	*He obtained the highest (first) marks in the examination and obtained a good prize (reward).*
twm ko kya myla—mwjhe tohfe ke təwr pər dəs rwpəe myle.	*What did you get ? I got ten rupees as a present.*
mwjh ko aj ek pwrana dost myla.	*I came across (by chance) an old friend to-day.*
məyŋ əpne dost se aj myla.	*I met (designedly) my friend to-day.*

When **pana** is accompanied by the inflected infinitive it does not take agent **ne**, and the sentence is often negative ; it then signifies " *to be allowed* " and often " *to manage to* " :

voh ane nəhiŋ pata (həy).	*He is not allowed to come.*
voh jane nəhiŋ pai.	*She did not manage to go.*
badʃa(h) ne hwkm dia ky gəvəiye dərbar meŋ aeŋ ləkin gane na paeŋ.	*The king gave order that the singers could come into the court but should not be allowed to sing.*
yeh qərar paya (or, yeh fəysla hua) ky jwrmana rəhe.	*This was settled that the fine should stay.*
ws ne goʃt tel meŋ ḍala ta ky voh səṛne na pae.	*He put the flesh in oil so that it might not be allowed to decay.*

ky : (*a*) a conjunction, often it means " *that* ": peʃtər ys ke ky voh jae, *before (this) that he can go* ; often it indicates a statement (noun-clause), like inverted commas : ws ko bolo ky ys vəqt fwrsət nəhiŋ, *tell him there is no leisure now (at this time)* ; ws ne kəha ky məyŋ jauŋga, *he said he would go.*

(*b*) When " *if* " can be replaced by " *whether* " it is expressed by **ky** : dekho ky ḍakvala aya ya nəhiŋ, *see if the postman came or not* ; ws se pucho ky meri koi cyṭṭhi həy, *ask him if there is any letter for me.*

(c) It represents the " *when* " or " *ere* " of abruptness or surprise : **voh thoɽi hi dur gəya tha ky baryʃ bərəsne ləgi,** *he had gone but a little distance when the rain began to fall.*

(d) It is sometimes used instead of **ya,** *or* : **twm yeh ciz cahte ho ky voh?** *do you desire this thing or that ?*

(e) It may take the place of **ta ky,** *so that* : **ghoɽe ko cwmkaro ky becəyni na kəre,** soothe (lit. *make a cheeping sound to*) *the horse so that he won't be restive.*

(f) It occurs in sentences beginning " *no sooner . . . than* " : **goli ka ləgna tha ky voh gyra,** *no sooner did the bullet hit him than he fell.*

VOCABULARY

ka **karxana,** factory	**zərd ; pila,** yellow
ka **meŋh,** rain	**bəyan kərna,** to relate (with
ka **zwkam,** cold (in head)	direct object, and **se** of per-
ka **malyk,** master, owner	son)
ka **məhina,** month	**khaŋsna,** to cough
ka **phaʈək,** gate	**xətm kərna,** to finish
ka **bəɣica,** small garden	**pəkəɽna,** to catch
zərur (without noun), necessary	**rəng pəkəɽna,** to become
zəruri, necessary	coloured
cahie, it is necessary	

EXERCISE XI

1. He sat down and began to tell a story in connection with the factory. 2. One man began to talk, another to read. 3. They began to converse among themselves. 4. Do you like this matter or not ? 5. See if there is a padlock on the door. 6. This task will take only a short time. 7. We began walking in the garden ; soon after rain began to fall. 8. He has got a cold, and coughs much. 9. It won't take more than three hours to come here. 10. He gave us leave to walk in his beautiful garden every day. 11. He does not allow his children to read such books. 12. The master gave him leave of three months. 13. The gate is open ; permission to enter is not necessary. 14. I did not manage to finish the task. 15. They were not allowed to lay a hand on it. 16. In front was a large tree and on it were many mangoes, some of which were ripe and some had begun to take on a yellow colour. 17. I looked everywhere, but no one was in sight.

LESSON XII

USES OF THE INFINITIVE

THE infinitive has a number of uses; it may be treated as a noun, or it may retain its transitive property of governing a noun. In either case it is liable to inflection like a noun ending in a.

1. When the infinitive is intransitive or without an object :

mera, or ws ka, jana (lykhna) befayda tha.	*My, or his, going (writing) was fruitless.*
mere, or ws ke, jane (lykhne) meŋ fayda nəhiŋ tha.	*In my, or his, going (writing) there was no benefit.*
mere, or ws ke, jane (lykhne) se koi əccha nətija nəhiŋ nykla.	*There was no good result from my, or his, going (writing).*
mere, or ws ke, jane (lykhne) pər əccha nətija nykla.	*My, or his, going (writing) had a good result.*
wn ke vəhaŋ jane pər bat qərar paegi.	*On their going there the matter will be settled.*
bap ka pwkarna tha ky ləɽka aya.	*As soon as the father called the boy came.*
mera ws se xəfa hona na mwmkyn tha.	*It was impossible for me to be angry with him.*

N.B.—The possessive form of the subject in these examples is necessary, e.g. mera, ws ka.

2. The direct object of the infinitive may be according to circumstances in (*a*) the uninflected form, or (*b*) the inflected form with ko or the sign ka. Where the infinitive is coupled closely with its noun, the direct object, it usually agrees with it in gender and number, but if a postposition precedes or follows the infinitive, then the latter must be masculine singular :

(*a*) jhuṭ bolna əccha nəhiŋ, səc bolna behtər həy.	*It is not good to tell a falsehood, it is better to speak the truth.*
yeh bat kəyhni mwnasyb nəhiŋ thi.	*It was not proper to say this thing.*
əysi kytabeŋ pəɽhni mwjhe pəsənd thiŋ.	*It was a pleasure to me to read such books.*
mwjhe ek cyṭṭhi lykhni pəɽi (pəɽegi).	*I had (will have) to write a letter.*

B *

(*b*) If the noun is followed by **ko** (direct object) or **ka**, the infinitive must be singular masculine :

ys kytab ko pəɽhna asan nəhiŋ.	*It is not easy to read this book.*
ys ɖali ko gyrana mwʃkyl tha.	*It was difficult to get down this branch.*
ys kytab ka pəɽhna koi asan bat nəhiŋ thi.	*It was no easy thing to read this book.*
kytaboŋ kə pəɽhne se ws ki aŋkheŋ dwkhti həyŋ.	*From reading books his eyes are paining.*
ws ko əfim khane ki adət həy.	*He is in the habit of eating opium.*
yogi saŋs zəbt kərne ki məʃq kərte həyŋ.	*Yogis practise control of the breathing.*

3. The infinitive is used as a future or a semi-polite imperative :

vəhaŋ kəbhi na jana.	*Do not ever go there.*
cori na kərna.	*Do not steal.*
xəyr, jao məgər jəld vapəs ana.	*Well, you may go, but come back soon.*

4. The infinitive is used in the inflected form with or without **ko**, with **ke lie**, or **ke vaste**, to express purpose :

voh mez pər khane bəyʈha.	*He sat down at table to eat.*
ləɽke khel məydan meŋ khelne (ko, etc.) gəe həyŋ.	*The boys have gone to play in the sports ground.*
voh mwjhe marne dəwɽa.	*He ran (threatened) to beat me.*
əwrət roʈi pəkane ke vaste ai həy.	*The woman has come to bake bread.*
voh bazar se səwda lene (ke lie) gəi.	*She went to buy goods from the market.*
gwnɖe ws ko piʈne ke lie ae.	*Hooligans came to beat him.*
vəhaŋ mwjhe lejane ke lie koi na tha.	*There was no one there to take me away.*

5. The infinitive is used to express intention, and being near to or about to. When the intention is positive the construction of the infinitive is with **ko** ; when negative, with **ka** :

məyŋ mədras jane ko huŋ.	*I am intending to go to Madras.*
məyŋ ap ki kytab bhejne ko tha.	*I was about to send your book.*

qwli ws ka saman lejane ko the.	*The coolies were about to remove his luggage.*
voh ydhər ane ka nəhiŋ.	*He won't come this way.*
voh əwrət vəhaŋ jane ki nəhiŋ.	*That woman does not intend to go there.*
həmare sahəb əyse nəwkər ko rəkhne ke nəhiŋ.	*My (our) master won't engage such a servant.*
voh mərne ke qərib həy.	*He is near death.*

6. It is used to express necessity. Here the infinitive is coupled with the noun and agrees with it in gender and number; the person on whom the necessity rests becomes the indirect object :

twm ko jana həy (hoga).	*You (will) have to go.*
twm ko jana pəɾega.	*You must go.*
ws ko jana pəɾa tha.	*He (she) had to go.*
mwjhe ws ko xəbər bhejni hogi.	*I'll have to send him information.*
twmheŋ wn ko cyṭṭhiaŋ lykhni həyŋ.	*You have to write letters to them.*
jytne kam kərne the ws ne kie.	*He did such tasks as had to be done.*
əwrət ko ag jəlani thi (or, pəɾi).	*The woman had to light the fire.*
əpne ymtehan ke lie mwjhe tin kytabeŋ pəɾhni həyŋ.	*For my examination I have to study three books.*

See further, p. 47.

7. For the expression of duty (" *ought* "), etc., see p. 46.

8. vala is often added to the inflected infinitive and gives it the significance of a future participle, " *about to*," or a noun of agency : voh anevala həy, *he is about (going) to come* ; təmaʃa dekhne vala (təmaʃai), *an onlooker at the spectacle (spectator).*

N.B.—vala is often added to nouns, giving a sense of connection or association : roṭi vala, *bread-boy, baker* ; pani vala, *water-carrier.* The noun is always in the oblique form : ghoɾe vala, *the man having to do with a horse* ; rwpəe vala qələm, *a pen costing a rupee.* It is not added to adjectives ; e.g. " *a good one* " is expressed by əccha, not by əccha vala, as foreigners commonly render it.

Vocabulary

ka əsbab, baggage, luggage
ka məwsəm, season
ka əfsər-e jəngəlat, forest-
    officer
ki bevəqufi, folly
ki nəyhr, canal
ki talim, education
ki sərdi, coldness
ki tarif, praise
fwzul, needless, foolish

gənda, foul
adəm xwr, man-eating
tarif ke qabyl, praiseworthy
swbəh səvere, early in the morn-
    ing
sərdioŋ meŋ, in the cold season
rəvana (*not infl.*) hona, to set
    out
jan dedena, to give up life

Examples

mwjh ko əpni tez(-rəftar) ghoṛi
becni hogi.

I shall have to sell my fast
mare.

voh kysi na kysi dehati ylaqe
meŋ bəsne (swkunət kərne)
vala həy.

He intends to settle in some
rural district or other.

ws ka yeh kəyhna hi tha ky gərəj
guŋjne ləgi.

No sooner had he said this than
thunder began to resound.

cwp rəho, twm kya kya bəkte
ho (kya bəkvas kərte ho).

Be quiet ; what nonsense you
utter !

Exercise XII

1. You must go home.   2. She is about to go home.   3. I
must buy a good horse.   4. Do not commit (kərna) such folly.
5. I do not intend to go from here.   6. Do not let him move
this baggage. Very good, Sir, I will not allow him.   7. To make
such expenditure is foolish.   8. There will be much benefit from
reading three pages of this book every day.   9. To drink the
foul water of that canal would not be good.   10. When do you
intend to go on leave ?   11. To travel is to get an education.
12. She does not intend to remain in this country after the cold
season.   13. She intended to set out, but did not.   14. There is
a man-eating tiger in that jungle ; the forest-officer intends to
go to hunt it early in the morning.   15. To give one's life for
another or one's country is praiseworthy.   16. I refuse to listen
to such nonsensical words.

LESSON XIII

CAHNA ; CAHIE

cahna, *to desire, wish, love*, is transitive.

    (*a*) **cahna**, *to love* :

maŋ bəcce ko cahti həy.	*The mother loves her child.*
ʃəwhər əpni bibi ko cahta həy.	*The husband loves his wife.*

    (*b*) **cahna**, *to desire, wish*, may take a direct object; the un-inflected singular masculine infinitive if there is no object or the object has **ko**; otherwise the infinitive agrees in gender and number with the noun it governs :

ap kya cahte həyŋ.	*What do you wish (want) ?*
ləɽki ne jana (lykhna) nəhiŋ caha.	*The girl did not desire to go (write).*
meyŋ jana cahta huŋ.	*I wish to go.*
kysan ne bij bona caha.	*The farmer desired to sow seed.*
zəmindar ne əpni zəmin ko becna caha.	*The landholder desired to sell his land.*
zəmindar ne zəmin becni cahi.	*The landholder wished to sell land.*
əwrət ek tez ghoɽi xəridni cahti həy.	*The woman desires to buy a fast mare.*

    (*c*) **cahna** may be followed by **ky** and the subjunctive :

məyŋ cahta huŋ ky ap yeh kam kəreŋ.	*I wish you would do this task.*

    (*d*) **cahna** may signify " to be about to," in which case the accompanying verb has the form of the singular masculine past participle :

voh cyʈʈhi lykha cahta həy.	*He is about to write a letter.*
voh gyra cahti həy.	*She is about to fall.*
yeh kam əb hua cahta həy.	*This task is about to be finished.*

cahie, *it is necessary, one ought*, is an impersonal form derived from **cahna** ; its past tense is **cahie tha**. Like **cahna** it may be used with nouns or verbs, and may take **ky** with the subjunctive. It can be used as singular or plural, but often **cahieŋ** is used for the latter ; **cahie thi** or **thiŋ** would be the feminine singular and plural respectively of the past tense.

twm ko kya cahie.	*What do you want ?*
həmeŋ sui dhaga cahie.	*I need a needle and thread.*
tumheŋ vəhaŋ jana cahie.	*You ought to go there.*
ləɽkoŋ ko əcchi kapiaŋ cahieŋ (cahie thiŋ).	*The children should have (had) good copy-books.*
twm ko bat ʈhik bətani cahie (thi).	*You ought to state (have stated) the fact exactly.*
twmheŋ kytab pəɽhni cahie.	*You ought to read the book.*
twmheŋ ys kytab ko pəɽhna cahie.	*You ought to read this book.*
twmheŋ tin kytabeŋ pəɽhni cahie(ŋ).	*You ought to read three books.*
cahie ky twm jəldi kəro.	*You must make haste.*

cahe (*2nd sing. pres. subj.*) . . . **cahe** . . ., means "*whether . . . or*" :

cahe choʈa cahe bəɽa meri bat koi nəhiŋ manta (swnta).	*None, whether small or big, listens to my word.*

cahe . . . **cahe** is exclusive ; **kya** . . . **kya** is inclusive :

kya əmir kya fəqir səbhoŋ ko mərna həy.	*Both rich and poor must die.*

xa(h) . . . **xa(h)** (*Pers.*), *whether . . . or*, is exclusive.

xa(h) məxa(h) (lit. "*wish . . . don't wish* "), means "*willy-nilly, perforce* " :

xa(h) məxa(h) ws ne wse həzarha galiaŋ swnaiŋ.	*He made him hear much (lit. thousands) abuse whether he would or not.*

Necessity :

Necessity may be expressed as in Lesson XII, 6 (by the infinitive with **hona, pəɽna**) or with the adjective **zərur**, *necessary*

(used also adverbially in the sense of " *certainly, of course* "), or
by zərur with ky and the subjunctive :

ws ko jana həy (hoga ; tha).	*He has (will have ; had) to go.*
ws ko cyṭṭhi lykhni pəṛi (pəṛegi).	*He had (will have) to write a letter.*
mwjhe cyṭṭhi lykhni zərur həy.	*It is necessary for me to write a letter.*
kya əmir kya fəqir səbhoŋ (səb) ko mərna həy.	*Whether rich or poor, all must die.*

The possessive construction also occurs, especially when the
infinitive has no object :

ws ka (mera) jana zərur həy.	*His (my) going is necessary.*
twmhara kytab pəṛhna zərur həy.	*You must read a book.*
zərur həy (tha) ky voh jae.	*It is (was) necessary that he should go.*
zərur tha ky voh jata.	*It was necessary that he should have gone* (for this construction with the participle, see p. 54).

Necessity or compulsion is often expressed by **məjbur hona**
(**kərna**), *to be (make) compelled*, and an Arabic accusative used
adverbially, **məjburən**, *compulsorily* :

məyŋ əysi hərkət pər məjbur hua.	*I was compelled to such action.*
məjburən məyŋ ne yeh kia.	*I did this under compulsion.*

Duty :

The sense of duty, propriety, may be expressed as in Lesson
XIII, (*d*), with cahie, and adjectives like **mwnasyb**, *proper* ; **lazym,
dərkar**, *incumbent*, or by such adjectives followed by **ky** and the
subjunctive :

twm ko kytab pəṛhni cahie (thi).	*You ought to (have) read the book.*
ws ko jhuṭi bateŋ nəhiŋ bolni cahie(ŋ).	*He ought not to utter untruths.*
twm ko bat ṭhik bətani cahie (lazym həy).	*You ought to state the matter exactly.*

The possessive construction also occurs, especially when the infinitive has no object :

twmhara (ap ka) jana lazym həy. *You ought to go.*

mera yeh kytab pəɽhna lazym həy. *I ought to read this book.*

VOCABULARY

ka səbəq, lesson	*ki* ɣərəz, object	mwmkyn, possible
ka gwna(h), sin, evil	*ki* zəban, language	kəm, deficient, little
ki yad, memory	*ki* koʃyʃ, effort	yad kərna, to remember

EXERCISE XIII

1. He is reading now ; he reads daily ; he likes reading ; he is in the habit of reading ; he reads at least one difficult book each month ; reading is a matter of joy to him ; he has to read much for his examination ; the pupil reads a new lesson every day ; he is learning yesterday's lesson ; one must read attentively to remember ; he reads only under compulsion. 2. One ought not to do evil with the hope that good may result. 3. You must read at least three pages of this book every day. 4. You should not strike your horse on his head. 5. She ought not to drink the foul water of the canal. 6. When do you intend to go on leave ? 7. I wish to learn the language of this country ; one ought to learn the language of the country in which one resides. 8. Whether he wishes or not he must pay this debt. 9. First you must make the effort, then it is possible success will come. 10. One ought to give help to others.

LESSON XIV

SƏKNA ; CWKNA

səkna and cwkna added to other verbs form conjunct verbs (see p. 59). They are intransitive and follow the root of the attached verb.

səkna, *can, to be able* :

məyŋ yeh kər səkta huŋ (tha). *I am (was) able to do this.*

məyŋ yeh kər nəhiŋ səkta (səka). *I can (could) not do this.*

Possibility is also expressed by mwmkyn hona and ymkan meŋ hona :

mwmkyn həy ky voh ae.	*It is possible he may come.*
mwmkyn həy ky voh aya ho.	*It is possible he may have come.*
ytna mwʃkyl kam mere ymkan meŋ nəhiŋ.	*Such a difficult task is not within possibility for me.*

səkna may be used to convey a sense of impossibility :

mwjh se yeh kam nəhiŋ ho səkta.	*I cannot do this task.*

Probability is expressed by an Arabic accusative formation from ɣalyb, *overcoming, prevailing* :

voh ɣalybən vəqt pər pəwhŋcega.	*He will probably arrive punctually.*
yeh rae ws pər ɣalyb hogəi.	*This opinion prevailed with him.*

cwkna, *to be finished with* ; it often has the sense of "*already*" :

məyŋ kha cwka.	*I have already eaten (dined).*
khana ho cwka.	*Dinner is over.*
jəb cyʈʈhi (xətt) lykh cwkuŋga təb ḍak meŋ ḍaluŋga.	*When I finish writing the letter I'll post it.*
jəb voh kam kər cwkega tab twmhare pas aega.	*When he has finished the work he will go to you.*
mərne vale ne kəha jəb məyŋ mər cwkuŋ təb yeh kərna.	*The dying man said: When I die, then do this.*

A sense of finishing is also expressed by xətm hona (kərna), *to be (make) finished* :

aʈa xətm hua.	*The flour is finished.*
ws ne thoɽi der meŋ kam xətm kia.	*He completed the work in a short time.*

xətm kərna (*to finish*) and ʃwru kərna (*to commence*), when used with an infinitive, have the same construction as cahna (see p. 45) :

ws ne kytab pəɽhni ʃwru (xətm) ki.	*He began (finished) reading the book.*
ws ne əpni kytab ko pəɽhna ʃwru (xətm) kia.	*He began (finished) reading his book.*
məyŋ ne hyndostani bolni ʃwru ki həy.	*I have started speaking Hindustani.*

Beginning :

ʃwru se.	*From the beginning.*
bat ke ʃwru (ki ybtyda) meŋ.	*In the beginning of the affair.*
ys məhine ke ʃwru se.	*Since the beginning of this month.*
əvvəl se axyr tək.	*From first (beginning) to last (end).*
na ws ki ybtyda həy na ynteha.	*It has neither beginning nor end.*

End :

bat (məhine) ke axyr meŋ.	*In the end of the affair (month).*
axyr ko ; axyr kar.	*At last.*
kytab (bat) ka xatyma.	*The conclusion of the book (affair).*
ws ne yntehai ymtehan dia.	*He appeared in the final examination.*

VOCABULARY

ka saman, stores
ka səwda, stores, provisions
ki dur, distance
gərmioŋ ka məwsəm, summer
kəi ; cənd, several, few

cəlana, to make go, drive
thək jana, to become tired
bəɽhna, to advance
məwquf kərna, to postpone

EXAMPLES

jytni jəldi ho səke.	As quickly as possible.
jəhaŋ tək jəld ho səke dəwɽo.	Run as quickly as you can.
jəld se jəld dəwɽo.	,, ,, ,,
voh həmari zəban bol səkta həy.	He can speak our language.
voh kwch kwch əngrezi bol səkti həy.	She can speak a little English.
twm mera lykha pəɽh səkte ho ?	Can you read my writing ?
syvae twmhare koi ys ko na pəɽh səkega.	No one will be able to read this but yourself.
twm kytni dur tək dekh səkte ho.	How far can you see ?
twm lykh cwke ho ?	Have you done writing ?
nəwkər səwda lene ja cwka tha.	The servant had already gone to buy stores.
mwjhe yəqin ho cwka tha.	I had become certain.

tehrviŋ sədi xətm ho rəhi thi ky ek roz tin admi ek jəhaz se wtərkər ʃəyhr ki tərəf rəvana hue.	The thirteenth century was closing when one day three men getting off a ship set out towards the city.

Exercise XIV

1. Can she go there to-day? She could not go yesterday to the market. 2. He kept trying to walk, but was unable. 3. This horse can run fast, but that one goes much faster. 4. Can you drive a car? If not, learn. When you have learnt, you will feel joy in driving. 5. In one day how far can you go? 6. He had become tired, so could not go forward. 7. Do not postpone till to-morrow what you can do to-day. 8. They had finished reading when I arrived there. 9. The stores are exhausted (have come to an end). 10. The summer is over; in a few days they will return.

LESSON XV

PARTICIPLES. CONDITIONAL AND OPTATIVE SENTENCES

Both the participles, present and past, may be used (a) as nouns, (b) as adjectives, or (c) in certain formations describing the state or the nature of the activity of the noun to which they refer. hua is often added to emphasise the idea of state or nature of the activity.

(a) The participles with or without hua as nouns:

dubte (hue) ko tynke ka səhara bəwht həy.	*For a drowning man the support of a straw is ample.*
ws ka lykha saf həy.	*His writing* (lit. *his written*) *is clear.*
mera kəha mano.	*Believe what I say.*
badʃa(h) ka bheja hua.	*The king's emissary.*

(*b*) When used as adjectives preceding the noun their full form is used : **gyrta hua pətta**, *a falling leaf* ; **gyre hue pətte**, *fallen leaves* :

roti hui ləɽki əpni maŋ ke pas gəi.	*The weeping girl went to her mother.*
dəwɽte hue ghoɽe nəzər ae.	*The running horses came in sight.*

N.B.—The past participle of a transitive verb with **hua** has a passive sense :

pwrane kaɣəz pər lykhe hue hərf həmeʃa ke lie saf nəhiŋ rəyhte.	*Words (lettering) on old paper do not remain clear for ever.*
əwrət ke pas ek bhəra hua ghəɽa tha.	*The woman had a full pitcher.*

(*c*) The participles are also used to describe the state or activity of the noun to which they refer :

(1) The present or the past participle so used may agree in gender and number with the subject ; it may be with or without **hua** ; further, the present participle, agreeing in gender and number with the subject, may be repeated, but without **hua** :

voh bəyt̪ha rəhta həy.	*He remains seated.*
ləɽki roti hui ai.	*The girl came weeping.*
ləɽki roti roti ai.	*The girl came weeping.*
əy ləɽki cwpki leṭi rəho.	*O girl, remain lying quiet.*
ləɽki dəwɽi jati thi.	*The girl kept on running.*
ləɽka pəgɽi baŋdhta (hua) aya.	*The boy came binding on his turban as he came.*

(2) The present participle may also be used singly or doubly in the singular masculine inflected form to show continuity of state :

əwrət ne syskiaŋ lete hue kəha . . .	*The woman said amid sobs . . .*
məyŋ mərte mərte bəc gəya.	*I just escaped death.*
voh siɽhi pər se gyrte gyrte bəc gəya.	*He just escaped falling off the ladder.*

(3) The past participle of a transitive verb when used to express state or nature of activity is always in the singular

masculine inflected form, for all genders and numbers, with or without **hua** :

mystri ara lie pəwhŋca.	*The workman arrived with a saw.*
ləɽka pəgɽi baŋdhe (hue) aya.	*The boy came having already bound on his pagri.*
voh paoŋ pər paoŋ rəkhe bəyṭha tha.	*He was sitting with feet crossed.*
voh nəzər nice kie bəyṭha tha.	*He sat with glance downcast.*

N.B.—The conjunctive participle, though often similar in meaning, implies that the action of one verb is completed before that of the other, and does not necessarily exclude a time-interval between the action of the two verbs : **yeh kəyhkər voh cəla gəya,** *saying (after saying) this he went away.*

The following idiomatic constructions with the masculine singular inflected form of the present participle should be noted :

wn ke ate vəqt yeh vaqe hua.	*This occurred on (at the time of) their coming.*
ws ke pəwhŋcte hi yeh hua.	*This occurred immediately (as soon as) he arrived.*

The participles are used in conditional and optative sentences.

CONDITIONAL SENTENCES.—The " if " clause (protasis) in these is introduced by **əgər**, the consequence (apodosis) by **to**, but often one or other of these particles is omitted.

1. Where the condition is likely to be fulfilled, or the question of doubt is not stressed, the indicative is used :

əgər mera bhai vəhaŋ həy to məyŋ bhitər jauŋga.	*If my brother is there I shall go in.*
əgər voh səxt koʃyʃ kərega to a səkega.	*If he tries hard he will be able to come.*
əgər voh gəya to paya.	*If he went, he obtained it.*

N.B.—If, however, there is an imperative in the consequence-clause, the subjunctive must be used in the " if "-clause :

əgər (jəb) voh bole to cwp rəho.	*If (when) he speaks, you keep quiet!*

2. Where the condition is less likely of fulfilment :

əgər dekhkər na cəlo to gyroge.	*If you don't look where you're going, you will fall.*
əgər hath kaṭa gəya to xun bəhega (see p. 56).	*If the hand is (has been) cut blood will flow.*
əgər ws ne kəcca phəl khaya to ws ko səxt dərd hoga.	*If he eats unripe fruit he will have sore pain.*

3. Where the condition is impossible of fulfilment :

(*a*) The present participle may be used in both clauses to express a condition present, past, or future :

əgər voh nehayət koʃyʃ bhi kərta to a nəhiŋ səkta.
Even had he made extreme effort he could not have come, or, *Even were he to make an extreme effort he would not be able to come.*

ytni kəmzori na hoti to voh kam xətm kər səkta.
Had there not been so great weakness he could have finished the work, or, *Were there not so great weakness he could finish the work.*

əgər hath kəṭta to xun bəyhta.   *Had the hand been cut, blood would have flowed*, or, *Were the hand to be cut, blood would flow.*

(*b*) The past participle of the main verb with the present participle of **hona** may be used in the " if "-clause, but of past time only :

əgər zəmin phəṭ gəi hoti to məyŋ ws meŋ səma jata (p. 59).	*Had the ground opened up I could have sunk into it.*
ws ne əb tak ws ka kam chwri se təmam kərdia hota məgər ləyla ne hath pəkəṛ lia (see p. 60).	*He would have put an end to it by now with the knife, but Layla caught hold of his hand.*
əgər məwt ne ws ka beṭa china hota to maŋ səbr kər leti.	*Had it been death which had snatched away her son, the mother could have been patient.*

N.B.—Distinct in use from this " consequence " **to** is another particle **to** which may come in any position after the first word of a sentence, and may convey the idea of " *moreover, however,*" or of a protest, but sometimes has no significance : **meri rae to yeh həy,** *my opinion, however, is this* ; **dekho to,** *just look!*

OPTATIVE SENTENCES :—These are introduced by **kaʃ** or **kaʃ ky,** *Oh that! I wish that!*   The verb may be in the subjunctive if present or future time is concerned, or in the past participle form expressing time present, past, or future :

kaʃ ky əysi bat na ho.	*Oh that such may not be the case !*
kaʃ voh ae.	*Would that he would come !*
kaʃ ky yeh vaqya na hota.	*Oh that this event had not taken (would not take) place !*

VOCABULARY

ka təsma, strap

ki peṭi, waist-belt

ki kwlhaɽi, axe

ki dhup, sunshine

ki həva, wind, air

lapərva, carefree

ghurna, to gaze

cyllana, to shout

cəɽhna, to climb, mount

EXAMPLES

kytab pəɽhte pəɽhte voh so gəya.	*He fell asleep while reading the book.*
bhure rəng ka koṭ əwr ws ke jəvab meŋ ek bhuri ṭopi pəyhne hue voh bhitər aya.	*Wearing a brown coat and a brown hat to match, he came inside.*
əwrət hath meŋ ləymp lie hue ai.	*The woman came with a lamp in her hand.*
voh bədhəvas hokər baɣ ki tərəf dəwɽi gəi.	*Distracted she ran towards the garden.*
phul nəsim meŋ ləyhrate ləyhrate nəzər ate the.	*Flowers appeared waving in the breeze.*
yeh ws ki mwŋh bolti murət həy.	*This figure is a speaking likeness of him.*
voh ləɽki ws ki mwŋh boli bəyhn həy.	*That girl is his adopted sister.*
voh nəya suṭ pəyhne hue əkəɽkər daxyl hua.	*Wearing a new suit he entered with a swagger.*
twm jəldi kəro nəhiŋ to voh cəla gəya hoga.	*Make haste, otherwise he will have gone.*

EXERCISE XV

1. Laughing and laughing she went away at last. 2. Fastening his belt and carrying an axe he came running. 3. Her eyes grew tired from gazing at the spectacle. 4. The man died in the effort. 5. She arrived with her hat in her hand ; afterwards, sitting in the sunshine she became happy and carefree. 6. Still

shouting, he filled the pitcher. 7. She went out wearing her gloves. 8. If he comes soon I shall go out; were he to come soon I would go out; had he not come soon I could not have gone out; oh that he would come soon! whether he comes or not I shall go out. 9. This had not happened had he come quickly. How could it have happened? 10. Come wind, come storm, I shall climb that mountain. 11. The servant came along with (ke sath; ke həmra(h) his master. 12. I wish my parents had been here; had they been here, none would have been happier than I.

LESSON XVI

PASSIVE VOICE

THE passive is not so extensively used as in English. It is formed by adding jana, *to go*, to the past participle of a verb, and both verbs are subject to the rules of gender and number, the main verb conforming to those of the adjective :

xətt lykhe jate the.	*Letters used to be written.*
xətt lykhe ja rəhe the.	*Letters were being written.*
cyṭṭhi lykhi gəi.	*A letter was written.*
xətt lykhe gəe the.	*Letters had been written.*
cyṭṭhiaŋ lykhi gəi thiŋ.	*Letters had been written.*

Frequently in a passive construction the definite object with ko of the transitive is retained :

pwlys ne ws ko thane meŋ ḍaldia.	*The police put him in the prison.*
ws ko hajət (thane) meŋ ḍala gəya.	*He was put into the lock-up (prison).*

The passive is sometimes used to express impossibility or inability :

qysmət se ləṛa nəhiŋ jata.	*None can contend with fate.*
yeh ws se kia nəhiŋ jata.	*He cannot do this.*
mwjh se əysi səṛi roṭi khai nəhiŋ jati.	*I cannot eat such rotten bread.*
əysi gəndi bateŋ kərne ləga ky mwjh se swni na gəiŋ.	*He began saying such foul things that I could not bear to listen.*

There are restrictions on the employment of the passive. The general rule is that it should be used when an agent is not mentioned ; e.g. " it was made by him " would ordinarily be rendered " he made it." But if the passive has been used though an agent was mentioned, the latter is put in the oblique form with **ke hath** :

voh dwʃmən ke hath təlvar se mara gəya.	*He was killed with a sword by the enemy.*

N.B.—**marna** may mean " *to beat or kill*," but the latter is usually expressed by **mar ḍalna** ; " *to be killed* " is **mara jana** ; " *to be beaten*," **pyṭna**.

In the following cases, where English may use the passive, Hindustani uses :

(*a*) An intransitive verb—e.g. **pyṭna**, *to be beaten* ; **kəṭna**, *to get cut* :

ws ka hath kəṭ gəya.	*His hand got cut.*
voh zor se pyṭ gəya.	*He was severely beaten.*

(*b*) A transitive with an object :

dwʃmən ne ʃykəst khai (pai).	*The enemy sustained defeat, or was defeated.*
ʃərir ləɽke ne bed (bet) khai.	*The bad boy got a caning, or was caned.*
ws ne təmaŋca khaya.	*He got a slap, or he was slapped.*

N.B.—**khana** (*to eat*) is used in combination with the following nouns :

juta khana, *to be beaten with a shoe*	**mar khana**, *to be beaten*
ɣəm khana, *to be grieved*	**gali khana**, *to be abused*
dhokha khana, *to be deceived*	**ṭhokər khana**, *to stumble* (se, *against*)

(*c*) **hona** with a borrowed Arabic passive participle :

yjlas kəl pər (tək) məwquf hua.	*The session was postponed till to-morrow.*
malum həy (tha ; hua).	*It is (was ; became) known.*
məyŋ ap ka məmnun huŋ.	*I am obliged to you.*
jəlsa sytəmbər ki bara tarix ke lie mwnəqyd hua.	*The meeting was called for 12th September.*

(d) For kəyhna, to say, call or name, in the passive kəyhlana, to be called, is used :

(voh) ws ko baŋs kəyhte həyŋ.	(They) people call it bamboo.
voh yaqub kəyhlata həy.	He is named Jacob.

VOCABULARY

ka xətra, danger, risk	ənpəɽh, unread, illiterate
ka ʃwmar, reckoning	həqiqi, real
ka titər, partridge	wdas, sad
ka kartus, cartridge	məʃhur, famous
ka ʃykari, sportsman	bəcna, to be safe
ka qwsur, fault	bəcana, to save
ka wzr, excuse	tuʈ jana, to get broken
ki yzzət, honour	səmbhəlna, to recover oneself
ki bhul, oversight, error	mwaf kərna, to forgive
ki lapərvai, carelessness	mwtəbənna kərna, to adopt

EXAMPLES

yeh kytab kwtwb xane se mere nam se nykali gəi.	This book was taken out of the library in my name.
haki khelte vəqt voh gyr pəɽa əwr ws ki ʈaŋg ʈuʈ gəi.	He fell while playing hockey and broke his leg.
zyndəgi vəhaŋ nehayət xwʃi se bəsər ki jati həy.	Life is passed extremely happily there.
yeh mərd ənpəɽh həy kyoŋky bəcpən meŋ bap ki məwt ke səbəb voh talim pane ke məwqe se məyhrum rəha.	This man is illiterate because in his childhood, through the death of his father, he was deprived of the opportunity of getting an education.
bəyhre, guŋge, əndhe tinoŋ ke sath həmdərdi peʃ ki jae.	Let the deaf, dumb, and blind, all three, be treated with sympathy.
cəwkidar ki aŋkh bəcakər voh bhitər gəya.	He entered, escaping the notice of the watchman.

EXERCISE XVI

1. The man was saved from the danger; he escaped the danger. 2. He cannot write or read, so must be counted in the number of illiterate people. 3. He stumbled against some

obstacle and fell and broke his arm. 4. Two partridges were killed with one cartridge by the sportsman. 5. What do they call this lad ? He is not called by his own name. This lad is not Sulaiman's real brother, he was adopted by Sulaiman's father. 6. Pull yourself together ! Don't be sad ! 7. It is proper indeed that he should be thought famous and receive much honour. 8. I did this by mistake ; please forgive my fault. No, this was a result of your carelessness ; you are only making excuses. 9. This is too difficult a task for me ; I can't do it.

LESSON XVII

CONJUNCT VERBS

THE roots of verbs are generally joined to certain auxiliary verbs, with which they may combine to form real compounds, in which case the auxiliary loses its usual meaning, otherwise both verbs retain their usual sense. It must be noted that if either member of these combined verbs is intransitive the combination is likewise intransitive.

The auxiliaries in most common use are **jana, lena, dena, wṭhna, peṛna, beyṭhna, ḍalna.**

jana: when added to an intransitive verb it usually contributes only a sense of completeness : **ḍubna**, *to sink* ; **ḍub jana**, *to sink down* ; **beyṭhna**, *to sit* ; **beyṭh jana**, *to sit down*.

ana and **jana** are commonly used with **celna** : **yehaŋ cele ao**, *come here* ; **voh wdher cele gee**, *they went off there*. **ana** is sometimes added to intransitive verbs and contributes a sense of completeness : **voh nykel aya**, *he came out*.

jana, when added to transitive verbs usually retains its own meaning :

voh cyṭṭhi lykh geya.	*He wrote a letter before going.*
voh bewht beṛa cenda de geya.	*He went after giving a very large subscription.*
koi ʃayr keyh geya.	*A poet once said.*

ana is used with its own sense in somewhat similar expressions :

voh rwpəya de aya.	*He gave the money and came.*
voh məzduroŋ ko wjrət (tələb) de ata həy.	*He comes after giving the workmen their wages.*

The last five constructions are similar in sense to those with the conjunctive participle.

lena : when joined to a transitive verb it contributes the idea of action directed inwards towards the subject :

yn amoŋ meŋ se chəy le lo.	*Take six of these mangoes for yourself.*
yeh cytthi pəṛh lo.	*Read this letter by (to) yourself.*

It is added to the intransitive verb **hona** :

voh ws ke sath ho lia.	*He accompanied him.*

dena : when joined to a transitive verb it contributes the idea of action directed outwards in another's interest, or of finality :

yeh cytthi pəṛh do.	*Read this letter out to me.*
ws raste se gwzro əwr yeh xətt ḍak bəks meŋ ḍal do.	*Go by that road and drop this letter in the pillar-box.*

Joined to the intransitive **cəlna** it adds the idea of suddenness or completeness :

cor ḍər ke mare cəl dia.	*The thief on account of fear cleared off.*

wthna (*to rise*) : it adds the idea of suddenness :

voh bol wthi.	*She exclaimed.*
voh betab hokər pwkar wtha.	*Becoming impatient he shouted out.*
voh ytni galioŋ se bezar hokər ghəbra wtha.	*Becoming annoyed with so much abuse he got worried (upset).*

N.B.—**pwkarna** when transitive takes agent **ne**.

pəṛna (*to fall, lie*) : it adds the idea of suddenness :

kytab fərʃ pər gyr pəṛi.	*The book dropped on the floor.*
kyʃti jəldi se cəl pəṛi.	*The small boat shot off.*

N.B.—**pəṛna** is used with the meaning " *to fall, befall, occur* " with pani, *water, rain* ; bərf, *snow* ; kohra, *fog, mist* ; qəhət, qəhətsali, *famine* ; əndhera, *darkness*, etc.

qəsbe meŋ əndhera pəɽ gəya.	*Darkness fell in the village (town).*
ws ki teori pər bəl pəɽ gəe.	*Wrinkles covered his brow*, i.e. *his brow became contracted.*

With the meaning " *to lie* " it is used of both animates and inanimates :

voh behoʃ zəmin pər pəɽa həy.	*He is lying senseless on the ground.*
jhaɽən fərʃ pər pəɽi həy.	*The duster is lying on the floor.*
dəfətən ws ki nəzər kaɣəz pər pəɽi.	*Suddenly his glance fell on the paper.*

bəyṭhna : it contributes the idea of completeness or suddenness:

voh təxt ɣəsəb kərke badʃa(h) bən bəyṭha.	*He usurped the throne and became king (by force).*
pərynd dərəxt se wɽkər zəmin pər a bəyṭha.	*Flying from the tree the bird alighted on the ground.*

ḍalna : it contributes the idea of vigour or forcefulness, e.g. marna, *to beat* ; mar ḍalna, *to kill* :

ws ne ek kartus se rich mar ḍala.	*He killed the bear with one cartridge.*
ys ʃiʃi meŋ thoɽa pani ḍal do.	*Pour a little water into this phial.*
ws jhəgɽalu zyddi mərd ne mera dymaɣ cəkkər meŋ ḍal dia həy.	*That quarrelsome, perverse man has set my brain in a whirl.*
ws ne əpni kytabeŋ bec ḍaliŋ.	*He sold off his books.*

N.B.—The single verb only is generally used in negative sentences :

twm ne ʃiʃi meŋ pani nəhiŋ dia (ḍala).	*You did not give (pour) water in (into) the phial.*

pəɽna, bəyṭhna, and leṭna are static verbs in that they have a sense of rest, not of action :

bərf zəmin pər pəɽi həy.	*Snow is lying on the ground.*
voh pələng (bystər) pər leṭa həy.	*He is lying on the bed.*
voh kwrsi pər bəyṭha həy.	*He is seated (has sat) on the chair.*
voh kwrsi pər bəyṭhta həy.	*He habitually sits on the chair.*

In the following combination both verbs retain their original significance :

ws ne fwlaŋ ko bwla bheja.	*He sent to summon so-and-so.*
voh əpne dost ko bwla laya.	*He sent for his friend.*
məyŋ ne ws ko kəyhla bheja.	*I sent word to him.*

VOCABULARY

ka həmla, attack
ka pərca, piece of paper
ka pənja, paw
əsleha (*pl.*), weapons
ki bədcəlni, misconduct

nice ; təle, below
əsleha ḍalna, to surrender
mwafi maŋgna, to seek pardon, apologise
nykalna, to put out.

EXAMPLES

mere dost ki begəm (bibi) behoʃ hokər zəmin pər gyr pəṛi.	My friend's wife fell senseless to the ground.
nəwkər ne səb cizoŋ ko mez pər rəkh dia həy.	The servant has placed all the things on the table.
meri ghəṛi taq pər rəkh do.	Lay my watch on the shelf.
ys pər hath ləgake dhəkel do.	Put your hand on it and push.
voh səb khana kha gəe.	They ate up all the dinner.
ḍaku ʃor se pəreʃan hokər cəl die.	The bandits perplexed at the noise cleared off.
juŋ juŋ məyŋ bəyhs kərta rəha tuŋ tuŋ ws ki zydd bəṛhti gəi.	The more I argued the more his obstinacy increased.
mwnʃi (babu) ne hwkm nəql kər lie.	The clerk made a copy of the orders for himself.

EXERCISE XVII

1. Take this for yourself ; take this to them.   2. Give me that ; give that up to me ; the enemy surrendered their weapons. 3. Sit down ; please sit down ; where may I sit ?   He is seated below the tree.   4. Put all these articles on the shelf in the cupboard.   5. The bandits killed her companion.   6. Has he written out the letters, as I told him ?   7. Throw out the water in this pitcher.   8. They all exclaimed : " We will not sit down unless you make an apology for this misconduct."   9. The dog has eaten all the butter.   10. Who has cut down that fine tree ?

11. Did those making the attack shout " Beat " or " Beat to death " ? 12. The monkey went off with the paper, but I snatched it from its paw. 13. Take your book ; I am giving it back to you ; stretch out your hand as far as possible to take it ; have you got it ?

LESSON XVIII

CONJUNCTS OF VERB AND NOUN

THERE is another form of combination in which one of the two constituents is a noun ; in some instances the latter combines with the verb to form a true compound and some other noun becomes the direct object :

məyŋ ne ws ko swsti pər məla- mət kia.	*I reproved him for laziness.*
cor ne ek bebəha zevər cori kia.	*The thief stole a priceless orna- ment.*

Some common instances of this construction in which another noun is the direct object are :

əda kərna, *to pay, fulfil*	qəyd kərna, *to capture*
ərz kərna, *to represent, state humbly*	rwxsət kərna, *to take leave of; dismiss*
bəyan kərna, *to narrate, state*	swpwrd kərna, *to entrust*
pyar kərna, *to love*	təjviz kərna, *to propose*
dərj kərna, *to make an entry*	təqsim kərna, *to divide*
dava kərna, *to claim*	təsəvvwr kərna, *to imagine*
qəbul kərna, *to accept*	təsnif kərna, *to compose*
qətl (həlak) kərna, *to kill*	yad kərna, *to remember*

In other instances the noun is not so closely combined and remains itself the direct object, the other noun being attached to it by ka :

wstad ys honhar ləɽke ki tarif həmeʃa kərta həy.	*The teacher always praises this promising boy.*
ws ne mwjh se hadyse ka zykr kia.	*He mentioned the accident to me.*

Some common instances of this construction in which the two nouns are joined by ka are :

bat kaṭna, *to interrupt*

bat manna, *to obey*

bat swnna, *to listen to*

bədnami kərna, *to defame*

dərxast kərna, *to request*

davət kərna, *to invite*

hyfazət kərna, *to safeguard*

xəbər kərna, *to inform of*

xwʃaməd kərna, *to flatter*

mədəd kərna, *to help*

mənzuri kərna, *to approve*

mərəmmət kərna, *to repair*

səyr kərna, *to tour, walk by*

təlafi kərna, *to make amends for*

tamil kərna, *to carry out (an order)*

tarif kərna, *to praise*

vada kərna, *to promise*

yəqin kərna, *to trust*

There are some combinations which can take either construction, with the direct object or with ka :

məyŋ ne cabi ko təlaʃ kia.
məyŋ ne cabi ki təlaʃ ki.
} *I searched for the key.*

ws ne wse ystemal kia.
ws ne wska ystemal kia.
} *He utilised it.*

kərna sometimes takes a direct object and is followed by the postpositions pər, se, ke sath :

kysi pər jwrmana kərna, *to fine someone.*

kysi pər ehsan kərna, *to show kindness to someone.*

kysi par ynayət kərna, *to do a favour to someone.*

kysi bat pər ysrar kərna, *to insist on a matter.*

kysi bat pər etyraz kərna, *to object to.*

kysi se məʃvəra kərna, *to consult with.*

kysi se səlah kərna, *to consult with.*

kysi ke sath əccha (bwra) bərtao (swluk) kərna, *to behave well (badly) towards one.*

kysi ke sath həmdərdi kərna, *to have sympathy for one.*

The following combinations with marna are frequent :

ws ne ʃərir ləṛke ko təmaŋca mara.

He slapped the bad boy.

berəyhm mərd ne bygəṛkər ws ke thəppəṛ mara.

The merciless man getting angry gave him a blow.

xəccər ne ws ke laʈ mari.	*The mule gave him a kick.*
saɳɖ (bəyl) ne ws ke siŋg mara.	*A bull (bullock) gored him.*
ek bhyʈ ne ws ko ɖənk mara.	*A wasp stung him.*
təyrne vale ne do tin hath mare.	*The swimmer took two or three strokes.*
vəhaŋ kəwn cəppu mar rəha həy.	*Who is rowing over there ?*
voh bəwht ɖiŋg marta hai.	*He boasts a great deal.*
ws ke ɖyl meŋ jəzbat ne joʃ mara.	*Feelings stirred in his heart.*

The following idioms with **marna** may be noted :

bəwht se sypahi jan se mare jaeŋge.	*Many soldiers will be killed.*
twm yəhaŋ kyoŋ mare mare phyrte ho.	*Why are you wandering about here ?*

VOCABULARY

ka ɣəyr mwlki, foreigner	*ki* təqrib, ceremony
ka əjnəbi, foreigner	*ki* dwlhən, bride
ka xwlus, sincerity	*ki* fərmaŋ bərdari, obedience
ka sərdar, chief	qabyl, worthy, fit
ka dwlha, bridegroom	məmnun kərna, to oblige
ka qəydi, prisoner	jhwkna (*intr.*), to bend
ka rəyhm, mercy	sər jhwkana (*tr.*), to bend the head (in homage)
ki xydmət, service (presence)	
ki gwftəgu, conversation	peʃ ana, to behave (towards)
ki ʃadi, marriage	

EXAMPLES

dyl hi dyl meŋ məyŋ ne ws ke sath həmdərdi ki.	Deep in my heart I sympathised with him.
ys bənd ki gəyhrai ka əndaza ləgao.	Estimate the depth of this dam (embankment).
fərz əda kərte kərte ws ne jan dedi.	He died doing his duty.
ws ne hysab nəqd əda kər dia.	He paid the account in cash.

C

ek rwpəya rezgi dijie.

Kindly give me change for a rupee.

yeh cyk toɽke dəs rwpia noʈ əwr reza dijie.

Please cash this cheque and give me ten-rupee notes and small change.

əy cəprasi, bəynk meŋ yeh cyk twɽa do.

Messenger, get this cheque cashed in the bank.

sərkar salana malgwzari bazabta əwr baqayda jəma kərati həy.

Government causes to be made the collection of the annual revenue regularly and orderly.

voh ws ko səcce dyl se pyar kərta həy.

He loves her sincerely.

kysi ne dərvaze pər dəstək di.

Someone knocked at the door.

bəŋgal meŋ hyndu log kali ki puja kərte həyŋ.

In Bengal the Hindus worship Kali.

eh mwsəlman nəmaz pəɽh rəhe həyŋ əwr xwda ki ybadət kər rəhe həyŋ.

These Muslims are saying their prayers and worshipping God.

voh cahta tha ky əysi sada myzaj əwrət se ʃadi kəre.

He was desirous of marrying such an artless (simple-natured) woman.

Exercise XVIII

1. He treated the foreigner nicely. 2. Do me a favour and post this. 3. I thanked him with sincerity. 4. He narrated to me the whole incident. 5. He obliged me by doing this. 6. He did homage before the chief. 7. He made him a promise, but afterwards broke it. 8. The judge imposed on him a fine of a thousand rupees. 9. We were conversing among ourselves about him. 10. Do you remember what I told you to commit to memory? Do you remember this? 11. Who will examine him? It is not yet known, but he will go up for the examination next month. He is strong in Hindustani and will pass for certain. 12. I do not believe this statement. 13. Assure him I will help him. 14. At the marriage ceremony the bride promised to love, honour, and obey the bridegroom. 15. The prisoner asked for mercy.

LESSON XIX

CAUSAL VERBS

(*a*) Many verbs have an intransitive form, which may be a passive or a kind of middle form indicating that something occurs of itself; a transitive; and a causal. The usual characteristic of the transitive of such verbs is medial a, and of their causal medial **va**. Some common examples are :

Intrans.	*Trans.*	*Causal*
bənna, *to be made*	bənana, *to make*	bənvana, *to cause to be made*
jagna, *to waken*	jəgana	jəgvana
nykəlna, *to come out*	nykalna	nykəlvana
khyŋcna, *to be drawn*	kheŋcna	khy(ŋ)cvana
pyʈna, *to be beaten*	piʈna	pyʈvana
khwlna, *to be open*	kholna	khwlvana
rwkna, *to come to a stop*	rokna	rwkvana

yeh sənduq səndəl se bəna hwa həy.	*This box is made of sandalwood.*
bəɽhəi, mere lie səndəl se sənduq bənvao.	*Carpenter, make me a box of sandalwood.*
məyŋ ne səndəl se sənduq bəɽhəi se bənvaya.	*I caused a box to be made of sandalwood by the carpenter.*

(*b*) If the simple verb is transitive, medial **a**, as well as medial **va**, makes it causal. Some common examples are :

dekhna, *to see*	dykhana, *to show*	dykhlana, *to show*
kərna, *to do*	kərana, *to cause to be done*	kərvana, *to cause to be done*
khana, *to eat*	khylana, *to cause to eat, feed*	khylvana, *to cause to eat or be fed*
maŋgna, *to want*	məngana, *to send for a thing*	məngvana, *to send for a thing*
pəɽhna, *to read*	pəɽhana, *to cause to read, teach*	pəɽhvana, *to cause to be read or taught*

wn ko kwch khylao.	*Give them something to eat.*
məyŋ ne wn ko nəwkər se kwch khylaya.	*I caused the servant to give them something to eat.*
wse ys kytab ko pəɽhao.	*Teach him this book.*
məyŋ ne əpne beţe ko məwlvi sahb se gwlystan pəɽhvai.	*I had my son taught the Gulistan by the Maulvi sahib.*

Sometimes the two forms of the causal of a transitive verb have the same meanings : kərana, kərvana, *to cause (something) to be done (by someone)* :

twm ne mwjh se bəɽa yntyzar kəraya.	*You have made me wait a long time.*
ws ne zəbərdəsti se yeh kam mwjh se kərvaya.	*By force he got me to do this.*

There are sometimes irregularities in formation :

bykna, *to be sold*	becna, *to sell*	bykvana, *to cause to be sold*
chwţna, *to escape, be let go*	choɽna, *to let go*	chwɽana, chwɽvana, *to cause to be let go*
dena, *to give*	dylana, *to cause to be given*	dylvana, *to cause to be given*
dhwlna, *to be washed*	dhona, *to wash*	dhwlana, dhwlvana, *to cause to be washed*
phəţna, *to be torn, burst*	phaɽna, *to tear, split*	phəɽana, phəɽvana, *to cause to be burst*
phwţna, *to get a hole in, boil*	phoɽna, *to break open*	phwɽvana, *to cause to be holed*
rona, *to weep*		rwlana, *to cause to weep*
sona, *to sleep*	swlana, *to put to sleep*	swlvana, *to cause to be put to sleep*
ţuţna, *to be broken*	toɽna, *to break*	twɽana, twɽvana, *to cause to be broken*

VOCABULARY

ka talyb-e ylm, student	*ki* atyʃbazi, fireworks
ka dhobighaţ, washing-place	reʃmi, silken
ka dhobipaɽa, washermen's quarter	məyhrum, deprived
ka nwqsan, damage	bəjna, to sound (*intr.*)
ka ɣwssa, anger	bəjana, to sound (*tr.*)
ki siţi, whistle	ys lie, therefore
ki mylkiət, property	fəwrən, immediately

Examples

ws tərkari ko kya kəyhte həyŋ.	What do they call that vegetable?
voh gobhi kəyhlati həy, əwr yeh phulgobhi.	That is called a cabbage, and this a cauliflower.
meri ghəɽi nəhiŋ cəlti; meri ghəɽi əcchi tərəh nəhiŋ cəlti ; ghəɽisaz se ws ko ʈhik (ki mərəmmət) kərauŋga.	My watch is not going ; my watch does not go well ; I'll have it put right (repaired) by the watchmaker.
bəcci ro rəhi həy; wse kys ne rwlaya; ws ko maŋ se təsəlli dyla dijie.	The child is weeping ; who made her cry? get her mother to comfort her.
fəvvara baɣ meŋ chwʈ rəha həy.	A fountain is playing in the garden.
ap ne meri jan bəcai, xwda wmr-e dəraz de əwr ap ko dəwlətmənd bəna de.	Sir, you saved my life ; God give you long life, and make you wealthy !
bazar se sygrəʈ bəyra se məngvao.	Have cigarettes brought from the market by the bearer.

Exercise XIX

1. This student read these books in school. He has finished reading them. His examination is over, therefore he will try to get them sold. 2. I am having my son taught Hindustani. He is studying this language diligently. 3. He got the tree cut down by a woodman who used a saw and an axe ; he then had it loaded on a cart which was drawn by a strong horse. 4. The woman had the clothes washed by the *dhobi* at his washing-place near his quarter. 5. You have kept me waiting full fifteen minutes. 6. The guard sounded the whistle and the train began to move out. 7. Get the washerman to wash these silk stockings with special care. 8. Send word to Joseph to come here immediately. 9. His cruel captor caused him to be deprived of all his property. 10. His dog has caused much damage in my garden ; draw his attention to this at once, and tell him I am very angry about it. 11. There will be fireworks in the park to-night.

LESSON XX

CONCORD OF SUBJECT AND VERB. COURTESY-TITLES

(a) When two nouns of different gender are joined through frequency of occurrence and ease of utterance to make a compound, the gender of the latter noun is usually adopted for both : dərs ga(h) (f.), *place of instruction* ; bəhi khata (m.), *ledger* ; ab o həva (f. sing. ; lit. *water and air*), *climate* ; roṭi məkkhən (m.), *bread and butter* ; cal cələn (m.), *conduct* ; ma bap (m. pl.), *parents*.

But the masculine may prevail :

xəzanci ke hysab kytab dwrwst həyŋ.   *The treasurer's accounts are correct.*

(b) When the subject, or the direct object in a sentence with agent ne, consists of two nouns of different genders the verb tends to agree with the masculine :

ləɽke ləɽkiaŋ ek sath khel rəhe həyŋ.   *Boys and girls are playing together.*

N.B.—Between two nouns usually closely associated the conjunction əwr is generally omitted.

(c) But the verb may agree, and usually does so in the case of inanimate nouns, with the latter in gender.

N.B.—Often in such cases where there are subjects of different genders donoŋ, tinoŋ (*all three*), caroŋ, or səb is made to conclude the expression and the verb is then plural masculine.

(d) The plural is much used to show respect :

jəj sahb ədalətga(h) gəe həyŋ.   *The judge has gone to the court.*

ap, hwzur, and jənab are always followed by the plural of respect ; likewise sahyb and miaŋ when used as terms of respect : bəɽe miaŋ, *good Sir!* When sahyb, or sahəb, indicates a man, a respectable man, the singular is used :

koi sahəb bahər həy.   *There is a man outside.*

sahyb is often used in Persian compounds : sahyb-e kəmal, sahəb kəmal, *perfect, one having excellence.*

(e) When the subject is a plural concrete noun or a pronoun in the plural, a concrete noun in the predicate must also be plural :

twm ws ke beṭe ho ? *Are you his son ?*

(f) When two nouns are commonly used together without əwr, generally only the second is put in the oblique plural, but if əwr is used both are generally in the oblique form : ləṛke ləṛkioŋ ko, *to boys and girls.*

ap, a pronoun, is used in two ways :

(a) When signifying "*self*" it is attached to a personal pronoun : **məyŋ ap jauŋga, ap jauŋga,** *I'll go myself.*
The Persian reflexive pronoun **xwd** is frequently used instead of ap : **məyŋ xwd jauŋga,** *I'll go myself* ; **xwd bəxwd** means "*of one's own accord, of itself.*"

(b) It is commonly used in a respectful or honorific sense, like "*Sir,*" and in such instances the verb accompanying is in the third person plural or the polite form of the imperative :

əgər ap zəra təklif kərke jəlse meŋ jaeŋge to vəhaŋ səb log wṭhkər ap ki yzzət kəreŋge.	*If you, Sir, will be so good as to go into the meeting, all will rise to honour you.*

Courtesy-titles and phrases abound ; the last example may be rendered in terms indicating great respect and yet in language in daily circulation (**rozmərra**) :

əgər jənab zəra təklif fərmakər jəlse meŋ təʃrif le jaeŋge to təmam hazyrin wṭhkər ap ki yzzət kəreŋge.	*If you, Sir, will kindly take your honoured presence into the meeting, all present will rise to honour you.*

fərmana is thus used in place of **kəyhna** (*to say*) and **kərna** (*to do*).

Among courtesy-titles are : **sahyb, sahəb ! hwzur !** *Sir !* **ap log ! ap hazyrin ! həzrat !** *Gentlemen !* **myssahb,** *miss* ; **memsahb,** *lady* (*of the house*) ; **mem** (from *ma'am*) **log,** *the ladies*—are designations current among Europeans.

ap occurs in a few common expressions : **ap se, ap se ap, əpne ap se,** *of one's own accord.*

apa, a form of ap, *self*, occurs often in the expression :

voh xwʃi (rənj) meŋ ape se bahər hua.	*He was beside himself through joy (grief).*

VOCABULARY

ka khet, field
ka chəkɽa, bullock-cart
ka mwrəbbi, patron
ka ohda, position, post
ka vətən, native land
ka vətən dost, patriot
ka mwddəi, plaintiff
ka mwdda ələy, accused
ka naʃta, breakfast
ki naʃpati, pear

ki wngli, finger
ki peʃgi, advance (money)
ki syfaryʃ, recommendation
ki syhhət, health
ki bəyl gaɽi, bullock-cart
ki xatyr, for the sake of
mayus, despairing, sad
cərna, to graze
təy kərna, to solve ; traverse

EXAMPLES

hər qysm ke pərynd nər mada dono(ŋ) cyɽia xane meŋ məwjud həyŋ.

Birds of every kind, both male and female, are in the Zoo.

yəhaŋ am, seb əwr naʃpatiaŋ pəyda hoti həyŋ.

Mangoes, apples, and pears are produced here.

yeh məkanat ws ke ʃərif xandan ki yadgar həyŋ.

These mansions are a memorial to his noble family.

mərd əwrəteŋ əwr bal bəcce səb məwjud həyŋ.

Men, women, and children are all present.

kəl ap aoge ?

Will you come yourself to-morrow ?

ap kəl aeŋge ?

Will you, Sir, come to-morrow ?

adab, ap ka myzaj kəysa həy.

My respects ! How do you do, Sir ?

ap ki təbiət kəysi həy.

How do you do, Sir ?

ɣərib pərvər, mwjh xaksar ərzkwnynda pər ynayət fərmaie.

Nurturer of the poor, render your humble petitioner a favour !

ws ne əpne dyl meŋ kəha.

He said to himself.

twm ne əpni cyʈʈhi lykhi həy ?

Have you written your letter ?

yeh twmhara kəwn həy—yeh mera əpna bhai həy.

What relation is this person to you ? He is my own brother.

" nənge xənjər se əpna kam
təmam kərna."

əwrəteŋ əpne bəccoŋ ko palti
həyŋ.

yeh mera əpna caqu həy jys se
məyŋ kam leta huŋ.

" And one's quietus take with
a bare bodkin."

The women nurture their own
children.

This is my own pen-knife I
use.

EXERCISE XX

1. Are you his son ? His sons and daughters are all here.
2. Horses and cows graze together in the same field. 3. My son
and my daughter, listen to me (my word). 4. Mangoes and
pears I like very much. 5. Her hands and fingers are beautiful.
6. Bullocks, not cows, draw carts in India. 7. I am going there
myself this very day. 8. If he himself cannot give the money
perhaps his brother will be able to advance it for him. 9. The
people returned to their respective homes. 10. Sir, you are my
patron—do me a favour by recommending me for that post.
11. Sir, do me a kindness and help me to solve this problem.
12. Every patriot considers his homeland as the best of all
lands. 13. My friend has gone to his village for the sake of his
health. 14. The plaintiff went away happy from the court, but
the accused remained behind sad. 15. There is a poor man at
your gate, Sir. 16. Taking into consideration his conduct I
will not give him a loan. 17. Sir, the morning meal, which the
English call breakfast, is ready. 18. Sir, you are (as) my
parents—help me in this condition of misfortune.

LESSON XXI

THE ENGLISH VERBS : HAVE ; GET ; LOSE ; BREAK

Have : there is no corresponding verb in Hindustani ; recourse
must be had to the following methods of rendering it :

(a) in the case of a transferable possession, **ke pas** is used with
the owner :

ws ke (mere, twmhare, həmare)   *He has (I, you, we have) a pen-*
pas ek caqu həy.   *knife.*

c *

(*b*) In the case of a non-transferable possession, (1) the **ka** of possession is used, or (2) an old form of possessive, **ke** :

(1) ws ki ek beṭi həy.   *He has a daughter.*

N.B.—In this construction some word is emphasised, "he" or "daughter."

ws ka ek bəyhnoi əwr ek damad həy.	*He has a brother-in-law and a son-in-law.*
mera (twmhara, həmara) ek beṭa həy.	*I (you, we) have a son.*
(2) ws ke koi beṭa nəhiŋ tha.	*He had no son.*
ws ki koi əwlad həy ?	*Has he any children ?*

N.B.—Arabic **valad**, *son*, plural **əwlad** ; the latter is used as a feminine singular in Hindustani.

(2) In the case of immovable property both constructions are used, i.e. with **ke pas** and the **ka** of possession :

ws ke pas tin bighe zəmin həy.	*He owns three bighas of land*
ws ki tin bighe zəmin həy.	„ „ „

(3) When a statement is made about a relative so that the emphasis is not on possession, **ka** is used :

ws ka ek beṭa həmare afys meŋ həy.   *He has a son in our office.*

(*c*) In the case of an abstract noun as the possessed, the indirect object is used :

ws ko fwrsət nəhiŋ həy.   *He is not at leisure.*

(*d*) In the case of members of the body, the construction with **ka** of possession is used :

ws ki aŋkheŋ nili həyŋ.   *His eyes are blue.*

(*e*) In the case of an inanimate possessor, an impersonal construction is used with **meŋ** :

ws ke ghər meŋ ek xub arasta gol kəmra həy.	*His house has a beautifully arranged drawing-room.*
ys təiyara-bərdar jəhaz meŋ səw ek həvai jəhazoŋ ke lie gwnjayʃ həy.	*This aircraft-carrier has space for about a hundred planes.*

ys bəmbar həvai jəhaz ke ynjən meŋ bəla ki qwvvət həy.	*The engine of this bomber has tremendous (calamitous) strength.*

Get : this may be rendered by **pana** or **hasyl kərna**, if effort or purposive action is involved ; by **mylna**, if there is the idea of its being a casual or effortless occurrence.

pana, *to get, find* ; **hasyl kərna,** *to obtain, procure* (see also p. 38) :

məyŋ ne əpni khoi hui cabi ko bəwht ḍhuŋḍha jəb tək ky ws ko nəhiŋ paya.	*I searched for my lost key until I found it.*
ws ne əyse əml se nehayət yzzət pai (hasyl ki).	*He obtained great kudos from such action.*
fwlaŋ dərsga(h) meŋ ws ne talim pai əwr sənəd hasyl ki.	*He got his education and obtained his diploma in such and such an institution.*

mylna, *to get by chance, meet, resemble,* is used as follows :

(*a*) With the indirect object it means " *to get by chance* " :

salgyrəh ke dyn mwjhe ek wmda kytab myli.	*On my birthday I got a splendid book.*
aj mwjh ko baɣ meŋ ek pwrana dost myla.	*I came across an old friend in the Gardens to-day.*

(*b*) With se, it means " *to meet with, pay a visit to* " :

aj məyŋ əpne fwlaŋ pwrane dost se myla.	*To-day I met by appointment my old friend So-and-so.*

(*c*) With se, it may also mean " *to resemble,*" and in this case jwlna is often added as a jingling appositive :

yeh ws se mylta (jwlta) həy.	*This resembles that.*

The conjunctive participle, **mylkar,** may be rendered " *together* " :

səb ʃagyrd mylkər khaeŋge.	*The pupils will all eat together.*

The transitive of **mylna** is **mylana**, *to cause to meet, mix, introduce* :

dəva meŋ thoṛa pani mylao.	*Mix a little water with the medicine.*
yn donoŋ ko mylao.	*Mix these two.*
hath mylakər voh jəld pwrane dostoŋ ki tərəh bat cit kərne ləge.	*They shook hands and soon began to converse like old friends.*
mwjhe wn se mylaie.	*Please introduce me to him (them).*

Lose, Break : in the case of **khona**, *to lose*, and **toṛna**, *to break*, cull (*flowers*), the forms **kho jana** and **ṭuṭ jana** are used to express unintentional occurrence, a kind of middle voice (*to lose oneself*; *go and get broken*) :

ləkəṛhare ne ṭəyhni ko toṛ dia.	*The woodman broke off the branch.*
meri cabi khoi gəi.	*My key has been lost.*
meri cabi kho gəi.	*My key is lost (missing).*
sypahi ki rəyfl saf (bylkwl) khoi gəi.	*The sepoy's rifle was completely lost.*
jo caqu məyŋ ne twm ko dia həy, xəbərdar ws ko na khona.	*Take care not to lose the penknife I gave you.*

The following renderings of " *to lose* " should be noted : **rasta bhul jana**, *to forget* (*lose*) *the way* ; **harna**, *to lose in a game*, like **jitna**, *to win in a game*, does not take **ne** if there is no object, and may or may not take **ne** if the object is **bazi**, *game*, or **ʃərt**, *bet* ; **dəm ṭuṭna**, *to lose one's breath* ; **hymmət harna**, *to lose courage, become dispirited* :

ʃəyhr se ate hue voh ra(h) bhul gəya.	*He lost his way while coming from the city.*
meri cabi bhul gəi.	*My key has been forgotten.*
məyŋ cabi bhul gəya.	*I have forgotten the key.*
wn ki hymmət ṭuṭ gəi.	*Their courage was broken (lost).*
voh hymmət har gəe.	*They lost courage.*
ws ne jue meŋ bəwht rwpia har dia həy.	*He has lost much money in gambling.*

ws ka dəm ʈuʈ gəya tha (voh bedəm pəɽa) lekyn voh jəldi taza dəm hogəya əwr ek dəm sidhi ra(h) lekər age bəɽha.

He lost his breath, but quickly recovered it again, and taking a completely straight road went ahead.

ghoɽe se gyr kər ws ka paoŋ ʈuʈ gəya.

He fell off his horse and broke his leg.

Vocabulary

ka cəppu, oar
ka cəwrasta, crossroads
ka cəwraha, crossroads
ki hath ghəɽi, wrist watch
ki ɖənɖi, pole, shaft

ki rəzaməndi, contentment
ki qənaət, contentment
ki ɣənimət, boon
ki mwlaqat, meeting (with)

Examples

əgər voh myle to məyŋ ws se səmjhuŋga.

If I come across him I'll have it out with him (settle accounts with him) !

əgər voh myle to məyŋ ws ko ʈhik kəruŋga.

If I meet him I'll deal with him !

əgər voh myle to məyŋ ws ki mərəmmət kəruŋga.

If I meet him I'll give him a dressing-down !

baz qysm ke janvəroŋ ke dwm nəhiŋ hoti.

Some animals have no tail.

wn ke pas do do suʈ həyŋ.

They have two suits apiece.

məyŋ yqrar pər daroɣe se myluŋga.

I will meet the steward by appointment.

sərhədvali bheɽoŋ ki dwm moʈi hoti həy, jys meŋ bəwht si cərbi hoti həy.

The tail of the frontier-sheep is thick, and has much fat.

əysi ʈhənɖi jəga jys ʃəxs ke pas na kəmbəl həy na cadər voh zərur kaŋpega.

In such a cold place whoever has neither blanket nor sheet will be sure to shiver.

mere ʈuʈe hue dyl pər rəyhm kəro.

Pity my broken heart.

ws ka kəleja mwŋh ko aya.

His heart came into his mouth.

ʃərir ləɽka khyɽki toɽ gəya.

The bad boy broke the window and went away.

ws ne ws ke ʈwkɽe ʈwkɽe (do ʈwkɽe) kər die.

He broke it in pieces (in half).

məyŋ ne əpni ghəṛi do pəyhr ki top se mylai.	I compared my watch with the noon-gun.
yəriboŋ əwr pərdesioŋ ko ys dəwlətmənd hijṛe ke haŋ se khana ya nəqdi mylti thi.	The poor and aliens were getting food and cash from this rich eunuch's house.

EXERCISE XXI

1. Do you have your own study-room ?   2. Have you a wrist-watch ?   Does it go well, or too fast ?   3. What reward did you get on winning ?   4. He got angry and broke the oar in pieces. 5. The horses ran away and broke the carriage-pole.   6. I met him at the crossroads yesterday.   7. When I get leisure I will call on you.   8. He has no parents.   9. Contentment is a blessing to those who have it.   10. He has enough, but not too much. 11. I lost my wrist-watch in the train two days ago.   12. Kindly introduce me to your friend.   Glad to meet you !

LESSON XXII

SA

1. The adjectival suffix **sa** (**si, se**) when added to a noun, or to the oblique form of the personal pronouns, gives a sense of "likeness," and the expression is treated as an adjective : **həyvan si surət**, *an animal-like appearance* ; **mwjh yərib sa**, *like poor me* ; **twjh sa koi kəmbəxt nəhiŋ**, *none so unfortunate as thou.* **həm sa** or **həmara sa**, **twm sa** or **twmhara sa** are the forms used for 1st and 2nd person plural respectively ; **ws ka sa** and **wn ka sa** for 3rd singular and plural respectively.

jəysa is similarly used but without **ka** : **ws jəysa calak admi**, *a cute person like him.*

Sometimes **ka sa** together are added to the oblique form of nouns : **kwtte ki si surət**, *a dog-like appearance.*

2. **sa** adds to **koi** the sense of " *whatever* " :

koi si kytab lao.	*Bring any book whatever (you please).*

sa added to kəwn has a sense of "*particular*," and kəwn is not inflected :

məyŋ kəwn si mez pər kayəz rəkhuŋga. *On which particular table will I put the paper ?*

When it is added to certain other pronouns the forms **əysa** (for yeh-sa), **vəysa**, **jəysa**, **kəysa** (for kys-sa) are obtained.

3. sa added to adjectives gives a sense of indefiniteness, like "*somewhat*" or "*ish*" attached to an English adjective, or has no significance : **ws ka choṭa sa sər tha,** *he had a smallish head ;* in **nənhi si bəcci** (*a tiny infant*) and **bəwht se admi** (*many persons*) it has no significance.

VOCABULARY

ka **kənjus**, miser	*ki* **səxavət**, generosity
ka **caŋd**, moon	*ki* **caŋdni rat**, moonlight night
ka **ʃiʃa**, glass, mirror	*ki* **kwrsi; cəwki**, chair
ka **gesu**, tress	**kəmbəxt**, wretched
ki **cəmək**, sheen	**bədqysmət**, unfortunate
ki **rəwʃni**, brightness	**səjila**, elegant
ki **rəwʃnai**, ink	**kənghi kərna**, to comb

EXAMPLES

twmhara sa əqlmənd zəhin admi.	A wise, intelligent man like you.
yeh kəyse janvər həyŋ.	What sort of animals are these ?
ws ne ek bəṛa sa pətthər wṭhaya.	He took up a fairly large stone.
ek xubsurət sa barasynga nəzər aya.	A fine-looking stag came in view.
ek kali bhwtni si ḍəraoni surət.	A black, ogress-like frightsome figure.
yeh səb nəmune yəksaŋ həyŋ.	All these patterns are alike.

EXERCISE XXII

1. He is strong ; he is as strong and brave as Rustam ; such a strong man I have never seen ; none is so strong as he. 2. Let anyone come forward. 3. The sheen on (of) the brass was like the sun's brightness. 4. Though rich as Qarun the miser was wretched and unfortunate. 5. If an opportunity comes I'll accept it gladly. 6. His generosity was as famous as Hatim's.

7. He was as elegant as a picture-illustration.   8. Her face was
as beautiful as the moon on a moonlight night.   9. What chair
shall I sit on ?   Oh, on any you please !   10. Standing up in
front of the mirror she combs her snake-like black tresses.

LESSON XXIII

RELATIVE—CORRELATIVE

A CLAUSE introduced by a relative particle and followed by
another introduced by a correlative is a frequent mode of construction : **jəysa kəroge vəysa hi paoge**, *as you do, just so will
you receive*.   These particles are :

DEMONSTRATIVE		RELATIVE	INTERROGATIVE	CORRELATIVE
Near	Far			
Character-istic Sound } y or zero	v or w (t)	j	k (=Latin *qu* and English *wh*)	
yeh, *this*	voh	jo	kya ; kəwn	so
yəhaŋ, *here*	vəhaŋ	jəhaŋ	kəhaŋ	vəhaŋ
ytna, *this much*	wtna	jytna	kytna	ytna ; wtna
ydhər, *hither*	wdhər	jydhər	kydhər	wdhər
əysa, *of this sort*	vəysa	jəysa	kəysa	əysa ; vəysa
		jəwnsa	kəwnsa	
yuŋ, *thus*	tyuŋ	juŋ	kyoŋ	tyoŋ
əb, *now*	təb	jəb	kəb	təb ; to

The correlative **so** has been almost entirely replaced by the
demonstrative **voh** :

**jo ʃəxs dana həy voh kəm bolta
həy.**   *He who is wise speaks little.*

The correlatives are sometimes omitted.

The pronominal adjectives əysa, vəysa, jəysa, kəysa ; ytna, wtna, jytna, kytna agree with their noun. They are also used in this uninflected form as adverbs ; the inflected forms əyse, vəyse, jəyse, kəyse are used adverbially :

jəysa (jəyse) kəroge vəysa (vəyse) paoge.	*As you act, so will you receive.*

N.B.—(a) To express quantity qədr (*f.*), *power, worth, quantity,* is much used :

voh ys qədr məzbut həy ky . . .	*He is so strong that . . .*

(b) To express quality qysm (*f.*), *kind, sort,* is much used :

ys qysm ka təmbaku bazar se lao.	*Bring this kind of tobacco from the market.*

VOCABULARY

ka bədmaʃ, rascal	*ki* draz, drawer
ka taɽ, palm-tree	*ki* diasəlai, match
ka byl, hole, burrow	*ki* botəl, bottle
ka dhuaŋ, smoke	paoŋ ki wngli, toe
ka məxməl, velvet	mehrban, kind

EXAMPLES

jo ho so ho.	Happen what may !
jəhaŋ ʃəyhd həy vəhaŋ məkkhi bhi zərur hogi.	Where there is honey, there the fly too will surely be.
jo twm kəyhte ho (voh) səb səc həy.	What you say is all true.
jo kwch twmhare dyl meŋ ae (həy) saf kəho.	Speak plainly whatever comes into your mind.
jys ʃəxs ko twm ne kəl ʃəyhr meŋ dekha tha (voh) aj fəjr ko mər gəya.	The man you saw in the city yesterday died early this morning.
jəhaŋ gwl həy vəhaŋ xar bhi həy.	Where there is a rose there is also a thorn.
jydhər twm jaoge wdhər məyŋ bhi jauŋga.	Where you go I will go.
jəysa wstad həy vəyse hi ʃagyrd hoŋge.	As the master, just so will the pupils be.

The particle **hi** is often added for emphasis to most parts of speech :

Pronouns : **yehi,** *this very one* ; **vohi,** *that very one.*

Nouns : **ʃwru hi se,** *from the beginning* ; **vade hi vade,** *nothing but promises.*

Adjectives : **voh kytna (kəysa) hi zalym kyoŋ na ho lekyn ɣalyb nəhiŋ hoga.** *However oppressive he may be yet he will not prevail.*

Verbs : **voh jane hi ko tha.** *He was about to go.*
        ws ke pəwhŋcte hi. *Just on his arrival.*

Adverbs : **ʃayəd hi,** *scarcely* ; **yuŋ hi səhi!** *so be it!*

<h3 style="text-align:center">EXERCISE XXIII</h3>

1. Bring what knives and forks there are in the drawer.
2. Why have you not done what I told you ? 3. Like master like servant. 4. She is kind as she is fair. 5. He is so thin that his fingers are like match-sticks. 6. The cook whom you recommended to me is a great rascal. 7. At the foot of (below) the very palm-tree under which you are now standing is a snake's hole. 8. Where there is smoke there will certainly be fire. 9. There is not the same quantity of wine in this bottle as there was yesterday. 10. The officer gave a reward to the soldier who saved his life. 11. The cat's paw is soft as velvet.

<h1 style="text-align:center">LESSON XXIV</h1>

<h3 style="text-align:center">INDEFINITE PRONOUNS AND ADJECTIVES; EACH; ALL; ENTIRE</h3>

THE indefinite pronouns are **koi** and **kwch,** *someone, any.*

koi : (*a*) *someone,* and, as a pronominal adjective, *any,* is followed by a singular verb : **koi həkim yəhaŋ həy?** *is any doctor here ?*

(*b*) Its plural, **kəi,** *several,* always requires a noun in the plural after it : **kəi log kəyhte həyŋ,** *several persons say* ; but compare **kəi dyn ke bad,** *after several days* (see pp. 83-4).

N.B.—**koi** has also the following uses :

> **koi**, *about, nearly* ; with this meaning it is not inflected :
> **koi paŋc mynə̯t meŋ ao**, *come in about five minutes* ;
> **koi ek bərəs meŋ**, *in about a year* ; **koi dəm meŋ**, *in a few minutes.*

> **koi koi**, *a few*, as pronoun or pronominal adjective, with plural verb.

> **koi . . . koi . . . koi . . .**, *one of a number . . . another . . . another*, with singular verb in each case.

> **koi sa**, *any of a number*, as pronominal adjective : **koi si ciz**, *anything whatever.*

> **koi na koi**, pronoun and pronominal adjective, *someone or other.*

kwch, *something* ; when used as a pronoun it is followed by a singular verb : **kwch to həy**, *there's just a little.* It is also a pronominal adjective : **kwch lə̯rkiaŋ vəhaŋ gwr̯iaŋ khel rəhi həyŋ**, *some girls are playing with dolls* ; **kwch bat nəhiŋ**, *it's nothing that matters* ; **kwch mwzayqa nəhiŋ, kwch hərj nəhiŋ**, *no harm* ; *no matter* ; **kwch pərva nəhiŋ**, *no matter* ; *there is nothing to bother about !*

It has also the following uses :

> **kwch əwr do**, *give some more.*
> **kwch kwch**, *somewhat* ; with or without a noun : **kwch kwch rai to həy**, *there is a trifle mustard.*
> **kwch na kwch**, *something or other* ; without a following noun.
> **səb kwch**, *everything* ; with singular verb : **səb kwch təiyar həy**, *everything is ready.*

hər, *each, every*, is a pronominal adjective ; **hər ek**, *each, every*, is used as a pronoun also : **hər ek (ʃəxs) ko yeh wmed thi**, *everyone had this hope.*

cənd (adjective), *a few* ; also occurs in the combination : **dwnya ki zyndəgi cəndroza həy**, *life in the world is transient (for a few days).*

baz, baze, *some of a number* ; with or without a noun : **wn meŋ se baz (lə̯rke) dyler the, baz bwzdyl**, *among them some (boys) were brave, some cowardly* (lit. *goat-hearted*) ; cf. **baz jəgəh** (*f.*), *in* *some places,* the singular being used sometimes after indefinite adjectives.

səb (noun and adjective), *all.* As an adjective it is uninflected, but as a noun it may take as its oblique form səbhoŋ : səb (səbhoŋ) ko ys bat ka ḍər tha, *to all there was fear of this* ; səb qysm ki məchli, *fish* (collective) *of all kinds* ; səb tərəh se, *in all ways.*

təmam, sara, *entire,* are adjectives : təmam abadi, *the entire population* ; sare pəṛos meŋ, *in the entire neighbourhood.*

N.B.—The following expressions are common :

səb ke səb, *one and all,* with plural verb ; ḍher ke ḍher, *whole heaps* :

xərbuzoŋ ke ḍher ke ḍher mənḍi meŋ ləge hwe the.	*Whole piles of sweet melons were heaped up in the fruit-market.*

VOCABULARY

ka təjryba, experience	*ki* qəwm, people, nation
ka məlka, talent	*ki* əsl, origin, fact
ka moamla, affair	jwda, separate
ki məharət, skill	zəruri, necessary, urgent
ki əfvə(h), rumour	əsl meŋ, in reality

EXAMPLES

təmam ʃəyhr meŋ xwʃxəbəri byjli ki tərəh phəyl gəi	Throughout the whole city the good news spread like lightning
ws ki kərəxt avaz hər kan meŋ pəwhŋci.	His harsh voice reached every ear.
twfan ne sara zyla bərbad kər dia.	The storm (typhoon) destroyed the entire district.
jəb taun aega (təb) məwt hər gəli kuce meŋ chypi rəhegi.	When the plague comes, death hides in wait in every lane.
dəbi zəban se ek ne dusre ke kan meŋ kwch kəha.	In a suppressed voice each whispered something in the other's ear.
ys mwsibət meŋ koi na syrf əpna lehaz kəre bəlky əwroŋ ki xatyr əml kəre.	In this calamity let none consider himself only, but rather act for the sake of others.

| yeh xətra mwʃtəryk (am) həy, həm səb mylkər ws ka samna kəreŋ. | This is a common danger ; let us all face it together. |
| kya hərj həy ky voh ae—kwch hərj nəhiŋ. | What harm if he should come ? No harm ! |

EXERCISE XXIV

1. Anyone can attempt this, but not everyone has skill, experience, or talent. 2. Let everyone take part. 3. One said to another : Let us consult together among ourselves. 4. Do not trust any rumour whatever of this sort. 5. Whom God has joined in marriage let no man put asunder. 6. This is our nation's affair ; in reality it is of international importance. 7. What one sheep does, so do all the sheep. 8. Some like one thing, some another. 9. All my worldly possessions I entrust to you. 10. Whole heaps of logs were lying on the ground.

LESSON XXV

NUMERALS; DISTRIBUTIVES; MULTIPLES; MONEY AND COST

Cardinals :

1	ek	
2	do	
3	tin	
4	car	
5	paŋc	
6	chəy	
7	sat	

Ordinals :

pəyhla, *first*
dusra, *second*
tisra, *third*
cəwtha, *fourth*
paŋcvaŋ, *fifth*
chəṭa, or chəṭvaŋ, *sixth*
satvaŋ, *seventh*

Henceforward the formation with **vaŋ** is regular, e.g. :

səwvaŋ, or səyvaŋ,	from səw, or səy,	100
həzarvaŋ,	,, həzar,	1000
lakhvaŋ,	,, lakh,	100,000

8	aṭh	41	yktalis	71	ykhəttər
9	nəw	42	bealis	72	bəhəttər
10	dəs	43	teṇtalis, or	73	tyhəttər
11	gyara		tetalis	74	cəwhəttər
12	bara	44	cəwalis	75	pəchəttər
13	tera	45	pəyṇtalis	76	chəhəttər
14	cəwda	46	chəyalis	77	səthəttər
15	pəndra	47	səyṇtalis	78	əthəttər
16	sola	48	əṭhtalis, or	79	wnasi
17	sətra		əṛtalis	80	əssi
18	əṭhara	49	wncas	81	ykasi
19	wnis	50	pəcas	82	beasi
20	bis	51	ykavən	83	tyrasi
21	ykkis	52	bavən	84	cəwrasi
22	bais	53	tyrpən	85	pəcasi
23	teis	54	cəwvən	86	chəyasi
24	cəwbis	55	pəcpən	87	sətasi
25	pəcis	56	chəppən	88	əṭhasi
26	chəbbis	57	sətavən	89	nəvasi
27	sətais	58	əṭhavən	90	nəvve
28	əṭhais	59	wnsəṭh	91	ykanve
29	wntis	60	saṭh	92	banve
30	tis	61	yksəṭh	93	tyranve
31	yktis	62	basəṭh	94	cəwranve
32	bətis	63	tyrsəṭh, or	95	pəcanve
33	teṇtis, or tetis		tresəṭh	96	chəyanve
34	cəwtis	64	cəwsəṭh	97	sətanve
35	pəyṇtis	65	pəyṇsəṭh	98	əṭhanve
36	chəttis	66	chəyasəṭh	99	nynanve
37	səyṇtis	67	sərsəṭh	100	səw, or səy
38	əṭhtis, or əṛtis	68	əṭhsəṭh, or	101	ek səw (səy) ek
39	wntalis, or		əṛsəṭh	102	ek səw (səy) do
	wncalis	69	wnhəttər		etc.
40	calis	70	səttər		

N.B.—koi (uninflected) before, or ek after, a number makes it indefinite : koi səw admi or səw ek admi, *about a hundred persons.*

Use of the cardinals :

(a) The noun with a cardinal number may be in the singular or the plural, but preferably the latter : do beṭiaṇ, *two daughters.*

If the noun is masculine and ends in a, the plural must be used : ws ke do beṭe, *his two sons*.

(b) A noun denoting time, quantity, distance is generally in the singular : do məhina, *two months* ; donoŋ tərəf se, *from both sides* ; dəs rwpia, *a sum of ten rupees*—cf. dəs rwpəe, *ten rupees*, where the emphasis is on the number of the coins ; bara fwṭ tək ləmba həy, *it is up to twelve feet long*.

The oblique plural is used :

(1) with the units to express totality : caroŋ tərəf (se), *on (from) all four sides* ; nəvoŋ əwrəteŋ, *all the nine women* ;

(2) with certain numbers below a hundred : dərjənoŋ, *dozens of* ; bisoŋ, or korioŋ, *scores of* ;

(3) with certain numbers above a hundred : səykroŋ, *hundreds of* ; həzaroŋ, *thousands of* ; lakhoŋ, *lakhs of* ; kəroroŋ, *crores of*.

The cardinal is repeated :

(a) to express the distributives : wn ke pas do do rwpəe, *they have each two rupees* ; wn ko tin tin ane do, *give them three annas each*.

(b) to express "*at a time ; in pairs*," etc. : ek ek admi koʃyʃ kərega, *one man at a time will try* ; do do kərke voh cəlte phyrte the, *they were walking about in pairs*.

Ordinals : those ending in vaŋ have viŋ for the feminine, and veŋ for the masculine inflected forms : hər tisviŋ kytab, *every thirtieth book*.

Multiples : To express "*times*" gwna (*f.* gwni) is used : dwgwna, dwgna, duna, *twice the size* ; tygwna, tin gwna, *three times the size* ; cəwgwna, car gwna, *four times the size*. Thereafter the cardinals are prefixed : səw gwna, *a hundred times the size*.

N.B.—(a) Addition :

do əwr do car hote həyŋ.   *Two and two make four.*

(b) Multiplication :

do duni car hote həyŋ.   *Two times two are four.*
do tiya chəkka hote həyŋ.   *Two times three are six.*
do cəwka əṭṭha hote həyŋ.   *Two times four are eight.*

Money : ek rwpəya = solah ane = cəwsəʈh pəyse.

Cost : "*for*," denoting cost-price, is rendered by meŋ or ko :

yeh caedan kytne meŋ bykta həy.	*How much is this teapot sold for ?*
ys caedan ki kytni (kya) qimət həy.	*What is the price of this tea-pot ?*
ys caedan ke kytne dam həyŋ.	" " " "
ys caedan ka kya dam həy.	" " " "
ws rakhdan ki car ana qimət həy.	*The price of that ash-tray is four annas.*
voh rakhdan cər ane ka həy.	" " " "
voh rakhdan cər ane ko bykta həy.	" " " "
yeh nəməkdan bəwht qiməti (məyhŋga) həy.	*This salt-cellar is very dear.*
qimət pəyhle se cəwgwni zyada həy.	*The price is four times what it was before.*
yeh raidani bəwht səsti həy.	*This mustard-pot is very cheap.*
məyŋ yn cizoŋ ko səsta səməjhta huŋ.	*I consider these articles are cheap.*
ap ne yeh bərsati kytne meŋ (ko) mol li.	*For how much did you buy this waterproof ?*
dwkandar ne ys ko mere hath bis rwpəe ko bec dia.	*The shopkeeper sold it to me for twenty rupees.*
məkan bənane ke lie ws ko do bighe (byghe) zəmin xəridni pəɽi.	*To build his home he had to buy two bighas of land.*
ys mwlk ka rəqba dəs həzar mwrəbba mil həy əwr ys ki abadi təqribən paŋc lakh həy.	*The area of this country is 10,000 square miles, and its population about five lakhs.*

VOCABULARY

ka mənjən, tooth-paste	*ka* qədəm, footstep
ka sabwn, soap	*ka* mən, maund
ka ser, 2 lbs.	*ki* chaoni, cantonment
ka adh ser, 1 lb.	*ki* bəndgaɽi, closed carriage
ka xərgoʃ, hare, rabbit	*ki* nəli, tube
ka nəmək, salt	*ki* mwʈʈhi (bhər), fist(ful)

Examples

mwjhe dəs əyse bəhi khate cahie(ŋ).	I require ten such ledgers.
ws ne paŋc paŋc rwpəe dekər wn sat admioŋ meŋ pəyŋtis rwpəe baŋṭ die.	He distributed thirty-five rupees among those seven persons, five apiece.
cuŋky bəhar ke məwsəm meŋ baryʃ kəsrət se hwi thi ys lie fəsleŋ mamul se dwgni thiŋ.	Since there had been abundance of rain in the spring-season, therefore the crops were double the usual.
ws ke pas lakhoŋ rwpəe həyŋ əwr səykṛoŋ bighe bhi, ba-vwjud ys ke voh fytrət se na kənjus həy na xwdɣərəz na lalci.	He has lakhs of rupees and hundreds of bighas ; not-withstanding this he is not a miser by nature, nor selfish, nor grasping.
ys xəbər ka ek ek hərf səc həy.	Every word of this news is true.

Exercise XXV

1. There are ninety-eight horses and twenty-seven mules in this cantonment. 2. For the closed carriage two ponies are necessary. 3. For each person five bighas and a cow. 4. In each box there are about a hundred matches. 5. Bring with you one tube (of) tooth-paste, three pieces of soap, and a pound tin of tobacco. 6. All four of his rabbits made off. 7. In the basket are six fish and a handful of salt. 8. A day will come when you shall hear me. 9. His every step seemed to be a maund (in weight).

LESSON XXVI

FRACTIONS; MEASUREMENTS—TIME, SPACE, QUANTITY

For fractional parts the following are used : pao, cəwthai, $\frac{1}{4}$; tyhai, $\frac{1}{3}$; adha, adh, $\frac{1}{2}$:

pao (tyhai, adh) mil tək mere sath sath cəlie.
Accompany me for $\frac{1}{4}$ ($\frac{1}{3}$, $\frac{1}{2}$) mile.

For smaller fractions the appropriate ordinal with hyssa is used :
ys zəmin ka paŋcvaŋ hyssa.   *A fifth part of this ground.*

For fractional numbers the following are used : pəwne, *minus
a quarter* ; səva, *plus a quarter* ; saṛhe, *plus a half* ; ḍeṛh, 1½ ;
ḍhai, əṛhai, 2½ :

> pəwne tin, 2¾ ; səva nəw, 9¼ ; saṛhe bara, 12½ ; səva
> səw, 125 ; ḍeṛh səw, 150 ; ḍhai səw, 250 ; saṛhe tin səw,
> 350 ; səva həzar, 1250 ; ḍeṛh həzar, 1500 ; ḍhai lakh,
> 250,000.

TIME :—The Indian day-time is divided into four pəyhr of three
hours each ; likewise the night-time : pəyhla pəyhr is 6–9 A.M.
or P.M. The ghəṛi is a division of time equal to twenty-four
minutes, but is loosely used for an hour ; ghənṭa, *gong, bell,* is
used generally to indicate an hour-division.

kya bəja həy.	*What o'clock is it ?*
kytne bəje həyŋ.	
pəwna (səva; ḍeṛh) bəja həy.	*It is* 12.45 (1.15 ; 1.30).
aṭh bəje həyŋ; aṭh bəj rəhe həyŋ.	*It is eight ; eight is striking.*
aṭh bəj cwke həyŋ.	*It's gone eight.*
adhe ghənṭe bad ghənṭa (ghənṭi) bəjao (maro).	*Strike the gong in half-an-hour.*
yeh hath ghəṛi tin mynyt age (piche) həy.	*This wrist-watch is three min- utes fast (slow).*
swbəh ke pəwne (səva; saṛhe) aṭh bəje həyŋ.	*It is* 7.45 (8.15 ; 8.30) A.M.
ʃam ke pəwne (səva; saṛhe) aṭh bəje həyŋ.	*It is* 7.45 (8.15 ; 8.30) P.M.

N.B.—The only exceptions in the case of the quarter-hour
divisions are : pəwne bəje, 12.45 ; səwa bəje, 1.15 ; ḍeṛh bəje,
1.30 ; əṛhai (ḍhai) bəje, 2.30. It should be noted that saṛhe is
used with and after three : saṛhe tin bəje, 3.30.

aṭh meŋ dəs mynyt baqi həyŋ.	*It is* 7.50.
aṭh bəjkər dəs mynyt hwe həyŋ.	*It is* 8.10.
aṭh bəjne meŋ dəs mynyt.	*At* 7.50.
aṭh bəjkər dəs mynyt.	*At* 8.10.
ṭhik do pəyhr həy.	*It is exactly noon.*

SPACIAL MEASUREMENTS :

Distance : 1 kos = 2 mil; 1 mil = 8 fərləng = 1760 gəz = 5280 fwʈ.

Area (rəqba) : field-measurement is by the **bigha, bygha** ($\frac{5}{8}$ acre approximately), and **kəʃʃha** ($\frac{1}{20}$ bigha).

DRY AND LIQUID MEASURES :

Solids and liquids have the same system :

1 mən = 40 ser ; 1 ser = 2 lbs. ; adh(a) ser = 1 lb. ; pao ser = $\frac{1}{2}$ lb. ; chəʈaŋk = $\frac{1}{16}$ ser. ; səva mən = $1\frac{1}{4}$ maunds (100 lbs.) ; ḍeṛh səw ser = 150 ser (300 lbs.). The English equivalents are only approximate.

VOCABULARY

ka mwsafyr, traveller
ka kag ; kak, cork
ke məsale, spices
ki sətəh, surface
ki abadi, habitation ; population

ki ghoṛdəwṛ, horse-race
ki kyʃmyʃ, currants
bərabər, level
həmvar, level, even
səb se nəzdik, nearest

EXAMPLES

twm paŋc mynyʈ der se ae.

twmhare ane meŋ paŋc mynyt der hui (ləgi).

twm paŋc mynyʈ der kərke ae

məyŋ yəhaŋ tin bərəs se rəyhta huŋ.

tin sal hue məyŋ vəhaŋ gəya.

dərya ki tərəf tin mil əwr age bəṛho.

bicvale təlao se tin mil ke fasle pər jame məsjyd vaqe həy.

yn donoŋ ke bic meŋ cəwthai mil ka fasla tha.

You came five minutes late.

,,   ,,   ,,

,,   ,,   ,,

I have been staying here for three years.

It is three years since I went there.

Go three miles further on towards the river.

The congregational mosque is situated at a distance of three miles from the central tank.

There was an interval of a quarter-mile between these two.

bavərci ne bazar meŋ ḍhai ser dudh ek rwpəe ko lia. | The cook bought 2½ seers of milk in the market for a rupee.

ek bəj cwka tha. | One o'clock had already struck.

mwsəlman mərd əwr əwrəteŋ dono(ŋ) roza rəkhte həyŋ—hər roz fəjr se pəyhle həlka khana jo səyhri kəyhlata həy khate həyŋ—ws vəqt se surəj ke ɣwrub hone tək wn ke mwŋh se kwch nəhiŋ gwzərta—khana pani yəhaŋ tək ky sygrəṭ pina bhi najayz həy. | Muslims, men and women both, observe the fast of Ramazan; before dawn each day they eat a light meal which is called *sahri* ; from then on till sunset nothing at all must pass their lips ; food, water, even a cigarette is not permitted.

Exercise XXVI

1. This field is round, that square, but the surface of both is level.   2. Will the park-gate be open at 9.30 a.m. ?   3. He has slept on since 10 p.m.   4. The travellers were fifteen kos from the nearest habitation.   5. It was a two-seer bottle, but there was no cork.   6. This field is large and round ; it has an area of 5¼ bighas.   7. That race-course is twenty bighas larger than this field.   8. For this cake ½ lb. flour, a handful of currants, some spices, a little milk, etc., will be necessary.   9. My watch goes fast (slow).   10. They are ten in number.

LESSON XXVII

TIME, MANNER, PLACE, CAUSE, AND " KE " EXPRESSIONS

Time :

   (*a*) Adverbs :

əb, *now*

təb, *then*

aj, *to-day*

kəl, *to-morrow, yesterday*

pərsoŋ, *two days hence* or *ago*

age, *previously*

pəyhle,   ,,

peʃtər,   ,,

piche, *afterwards*

bad meŋ,   ,,

həmeʃa, *always*

bərabər,   ,,

kəbhi (nəhiŋ), *ever* (*never*)

kəbhi kəbhi, *sometimes*

kəhiŋ (nəhiŋ), *somewhere* (*nowhere*)

(b) Adverbial Expressions :

ws dyn (roz), *on that day*

ws rat, *on that night*

yn (wn) dynoŋ, *in these (those) days*

ys (ws) dəfe, *on this (that) occasion*

ys (ws) vəqt, *at this (that) time*

dyn (rat) ko, *by day (night)*

ytne meŋ, *in the meantime*

vəqt pər, *punctually*

ys (ws) vəqt tək, *till this (that) time*

rat dyn, *day and night*

roz, hər roz, *daily*

aj kəl, *nowadays*

kəbhi na kəbhi, *some time or other*

(c) Conjunctions :

jəb, *when*. (1) With a present tense it means " *whenever* " :

jəb voh git gata həy təb səb swnte həyŋ.

Whenever he sings a song, all listen.

(2) With the future or the subjunctive it is conditional, and its construction is like that of əgər (see p. 53).

təb or to introduces its consequence-clause. Sometimes jəb is retained and təb or to omitted ; sometimes jəb is omitted and təb or to retained.

jəbhi, jəb kəbhi (*whenever*) and joŋhi(ŋ) (*as soon as*) are constructed like jəb. jəbhi often means " *that is why.*"

jo is sometimes used with the meaning of jəb.

jəb tək may mean (1) *whilst*, (2) *until*. In the latter sense it requires a negative :

(1) jəb tək voh vəhaŋ rəha məyŋ bhi rəha.

Whilst he stayed there I too stayed.

(2) hazyr rəho jəb (or, yəhaŋ) tək ky məyŋ vapəs na auŋ.

Stay till I return.

(d) With ke : wn dynoŋ ke (se) pəyhle (peʃtər), *before those days* ; ws zəmane ke bad, *after that time.*

(e) Idiomatic constructions :

(1) " *Immediately on* " is expressed by the oblique form of the present participle, singular masculine, with hi : ws ke pəwhŋcte hi, *on his arrival* ; wse ys xəyal ke ate hi, *as soon as this idea came to him.*

(2) "*At the moment of*" is expressed by the oblique form of the present participle, singular masculine, with **vəqt**, *time* : **wn ke jate vəqt**, *at the time of their going.*

Lists of common time-expressions :

About:

rat ke dəs bəje ke qərib.	*About 10 P.M.*
swbəh ke nəw bəje ke qərib jəb məyŋ vəhaŋ gəya.	*About 10 A.M. when I went there.*

After:

ws vaqye ke bad.	*After that incident.*
zəra der ke bad.	*After a little (delay).*
ys faysle ke tin məhine bad.	*Three months after this decision.*

Ago:

car həfta pəyhle yeh hua.	*This occurred four weeks ago.*
əb se do bərəs pəyhle bəṛa twfan aya.	*Two years ago there was a great storm.*
kəi sal peſtər ws ka yntyqal hua.	*He died several years ago.*
do roz hue voh cəla gəya.	*He went away two days ago.*
kwch dyn hue (ky) voh aya.	*He came some days ago.*
yeh do sal ki bat həy.	*It is a matter of two years ago.*
ys bat (əmr) ko do sal hogəe.	*" " " " "*
mwddət hui yeh bəṛa pətthər gyra tha.	*It was long ago that this big stone fell.*

At, by, in, on: **dyn (rat) ko,** *by day (night)* ; **swbəh (ſam) ko,** *in the morning (evening)* ; **do pəyhr (ko),** *at noon* ; **adhi rat ko,** *at midnight* ; **bwddh ko,** *on Wednesday* ; **thoṛi der meŋ,** *in a short time* ; **wmr bhər meŋ,** *in a lifetime* ; **dusre ləmhe meŋ,** *next moment* ; **aj swbəh (ko),** *this morning* ; **ysi (wsi) dyn (rat),** *this (that) very day (night).*

Before: **pəyhle,** *previously* ; **pəyhle hi se,** *already* ; **hadyse se pəyhle (peſtər),** *before the accident.* (See also *Ago.*)

For : in the sense of "*since then and continuing*" is rendered by **se** ; in the sense of "*till then but finished,*" by **tək :**

tin ghənṭe tək voh əysa kərta rəha.	*For three hours he continued doing this.*
car dyn tək voh vəhaŋ ṭhəyra.	*He stayed there for three days.*

voh bəwht dyn tək yəhaŋ rəha.	*He stayed here for many days.*
der tək cwp rəyhne ke bad.	*After keeping quiet for a time.*
mere vaĺydəyn tin sal tək vəhaŋ rəhe.	*My parents stayed there three years.*
kwch der yntyzar rəha.	*The waiting lasted some time.*
məyŋ yəhaŋ do sal se rəyhta huŋ.	*I've been staying here for two years.*
məyŋ do bərəs se yəhaŋ huŋ.	*I've stayed here for two years.*

How long, etc. :

ap kəb tək vapəs aeŋge.	*How long will it be till you return?*
yeh cyʈʈhi yəhaŋ kəb se həy.	*How long has this letter been here?*
twmhari wmr kytni həy, bis bərəs se zyada ya kəm.	*How old are you, more or less than twenty?*
voh kytne sal ka həy—voh bəcca tin sala həy.	*How old is he? That youngster is a three-year-old.*

Near :

rəvangi ka vəqt qərib həy.	*The time of setting out is near.*

Since :

təb se kytne dyn hue.	*How many days have passed since then?*
do bərəs ki bat həy ky voh aya.	*It's a matter of two years since he came.*
ws ko ae do bərəs hue.	
ap ko ʃykar khele kytna ərsa hua.	*How long is it since you went shooting?*

Until, Up to :

cəwda dyn tək.	*Up to fourteen days.*

Age :

twmhari wmr kya həy.	*How old are you?*
kytne sal ki wmr həy.	
məyŋ calis sal (bərəs) ka huŋ.	*I am forty years of age.*
voh əpni wmr ke bisveŋ sal meŋ tha.	*He was in his twentieth year.*
dəs sal (bərəs) ki nəw jəvan ləʈki thi.	*She was a young girl of ten years.*
car sala (car bərəs ki) ləʈki thi.	*She was a four-year-old girl.*

Course, duration :

bat (gwftəgu) ke əsna (dəwran) meŋ. *In the course of conversation.*

ləɽai ke dəwran meŋ. *During the war.*

Last : gəe sal (bərəs), *last year* ; pychle (gwzəʃta) sal, *last year* ; rat ka pychla pəyhr, 3-6 A.M. ; pychli rat ki ʈhəndi həva, *the cool breeze before dawn.*

Morning : swbəh (ko), *in the morning* ; swbəh səvere, *early in the morning ;* fəjr ko, *at dawn.*

Next : əgle (dusre, aynda) sal, *next year.*

Night-long :

təməm (sari) rat. *The entire night.*

rat bhər. *The whole night long.*

voh rat ko bwri niŋd sota həy. *He sleeps badly at nights.*

Noon : do pəyhr, (*at*) *noon* ; do pəyhr hogəi, *noon came.*

Pass, elapse :

ytna ərsa gwzər gəya. *So long a period passed.*

vəqt bəɽe məze meŋ gwzra. *The time passed very enjoyably.*

dəs sal (bərəs) gwzər gəe əwr kwch nəhiŋ hua. *Ten years passed and nothing happened.*

Period : ərsa (see *Pass*) ; mwddət (see *Ago*) ; əsr : jədid əsr ke nəe xəyalat, *the new ideas of the new age.*

Time :

voh zəmana jəld anevala həy. *That time is quickly coming.*

vəqt kəm (mwxtəsər) həy. *The time is short.*

synrəsida, *aged.* buɽha ; bwɖɖha, *old.*

choʈa, *junior.* bəɽa, *senior.*

ədheɽ, *middle-aged.* jəvan ; kəmsyn ; choʈa, *young.*

Daily :   rozana təjryba, *a daily experience.*

Weekly :   həftevar əxbar, *a weekly newspaper.*

Monthly :   mahvari tənxah, *monthly salary.*

Annual :   kəmpəni ka baqayda salana yjlas, *the firm's regular annual meeting.*

MANNER :

(a) yuŋ, *thus* ;   yuŋ hi, *in this very way* ;   yuŋ hi səhi, *be it so then !*

(b) ys (ws) tərəh (tərhe).   *In this (that) way.*
    meri tərəh.   *According to my way.*
    yeh gwlabdan kəyse ṭuṭa.   *How did this flower-pot get broken ?*

(c) kyoŋkər (somewhat rhetorical in use) :
    yeh kyoŋkər hua.   *How did this happen ?*
    meri jan kyoŋkər bəcegi.   *How can I escape the danger ?*

(d) kysi na kysi təriqe se.   *By some means or other.*
    ws ne socte socte kam kərne *After much reflection he de-*
        ka təriqa nykala.   *vised a means of doing the work.*

Other common adverbial expressions :

    mərdana (*adj.*, *adv.*), *manly.*   əndazèn; əndaz se, *by guess.*
    sypahiana (,,   ,,), *soldier-*   ahysta ahysta, *slowly, gently.*
        like.   dəbe paoŋ, *with silent tread.*
    yttyfaqən; yttyfaq se, *by*   nənge paoŋ, *with bare feet.*
        chance.   nənge sər, *with bare head.*

Some adjectives may be used adverbially : voh əccha bolta həy, *he speaks well* ; voh jəld aega, *he will come soon* ; əysa ; əyse, *in this way* ; vəysa ; vəyse, *in that way* ; jəysa, jəyse, *in what manner.*

PLACE :

(a) yəhaŋ, *here* ; yəhiŋ, *in this very place* ; vəhaŋ, vəhiŋ, *there* ; kəhin, *somewhere* ; kəhiŋ kəhiŋ, *here and there* ; kəhiŋ na kəhiŋ, *somewhere or other.*

(b) ys (ws) jəgəh.   *In this (that) place.*
    əgər məyŋ ap ki jəgəh pər   *Had I been in your place.*
        hota.

(c) ys (ws) tərəf.   *In this (that) direction.*
    məyŋ kys tərəf jauŋ—meri   *In which direction may I go ?*
        tərəf ao.   *Come towards me.*

voh məndər ki tərəf se a rəha tha.	*He was coming from the direction of the temple.*
cəlo həm pwl se gwzərkər dərya ke upər ki tərəf chəy mil tək kyʃti cəlaeŋ (kheveŋ).	*Passing the bridge let us row the boat as far as six miles towards the upper reaches of the river.*

(*d*) dur (*adj.* and *noun*) : dur tək, *to a distance* ; bazar yəhaŋ se kytni dur həy, *how far is the market from here ?*

(*e*) The following words can be used as adverbs, or as postpositions with ke :

upər, *above*	pas; nəzdik, *near*	əndər; bhitər, *inside*
nice, *beneath*	bərabər, *alongside*	bahər, *outside*
age ; samne, *in front*	dərmiyan, *midst*	haŋ, *at the house of*
piche, *behind*	yrd gyrd, *around*	

CAUSE :

cuŋky; kyoŋky, *because, since.* When the " because-clause " precedes, cuŋky is used, and ys lie (*therefore*) introduces the consequence-clause ; otherwise kyoŋky is used for " because " :

cuŋky voh həŋsa ys lie məyŋ xwʃ hua.	*Because he laughed therefore I was happy.*
məyŋ xwʃ hua kyoŋky voh həŋsa.	*I was happy because he laughed.*

Other expressions are :

(*a*) ys (ws) vəje (səbəb) se, *for this (that) reason.*

(*b*) ys ke bays, *on account of this* ; dər ke mare, *on account of fear.*

With ke a number of Arabic adjectives (participles mostly) are combined ; the noun preceding is in the oblique form :

layq, *fit for.*	mwtabyq, *corresponding to.*
mwafyq, *in accordance with.*	qabyl, *worthy of.*
mwtəəllyq, *in connection with.*	qərib, *near.*
məyŋ ap ki səlah ke mwtabyq kam kəruŋga.	*I will do the work as you advise.*

Compare : **voh səza ka mwstəhyq həy,** *he is deserving of punishment* ; and a Hindi idiom : **voh bat ka səcca həy,** *he is true to his word.*

N.B.—Often the order of words is inverted to emphasise something : **yeh təmaʃa qabyl dekhne ke həy,** *this is a show worth seeing.*

Some other Arabic words are similarly combined (with **ke**) :

əlava, *besides*	xylaf, *in opposition to*
bədle, *in exchange*	syva ; syvae, *except*
həvale, *in charge, trust*	zərie, *by means of*
yvəz, *instead*	zymme, *in (one's) responsibility*

The following expressions should be noted :   (ke) **bare meŋ**, (**ki) babət,** *in connection with* ; **bənysbət ys ke,** *in respect of this, in comparison with this* ; (**ke)sath,** *along with.*

VOCABULARY

ka babu, clerk	rəsila, juicy
ka mwjrym, criminal	motəbər, reliable
ka qanun, law	pəyhnna, to wear
ka gəva(h), a witness	kyoŋ, why ?
ka ylzam, allegation, accusation	kysi ke nəzdik, in one's opinion
ki gəvahi, evidence	

EXAMPLES

jəb ghənṭa bəje həm bhitər jaeŋ.	When the bell rings let us go inside.
mərte dəm tək voh ys bat se ynkar kərta rəha.	Till his dying breath he continued to deny this.
joŋhiŋ məyŋ ohde ka yʃtehar kəruŋga dərxasteŋ pəwhŋcti rəheŋgi.	As soon as I advertise the post, applications will keep arriving.
vəfadar kwtta rəha jəb tək malyk vapəs na aya.	The faithful dog stayed until his master returned.
bənysbət ws xətt ke yeh zəruri həy.	As compared with that letter this is urgent.
ws ki xahyʃ ke mwafyq məyŋ ne əysa kia.	According to his wish I did this.

ys jəga ki ab o həva mere myzaj ke mwafyq həy.

The climate of this place agrees with my health.

məyŋ ys ciz ki hyfazət ka zymmedar nəhiŋ.

I am not responsible for the safety of this thing.

ys tərəf dekho, ws ki tərəf nəhiŋ.

Look this way, not towards him.

jəraym-peʃa log kəbhi nəhiŋ pəchtate.

Professional criminals never repent.

sən 1942 isvi mwtabyq sən 1361 hyjri ke.

1942 A.D., corresponding to the year 1361 of the *Hijra* (622 A.D.).

Exercise XXVII

1. I did not come as no one called me. 2. On hearing the midday gun we will set out. 3. Has the clerk come to office to-day ? If not, why not ? 4. When you sit in the sun wear your hat, otherwise you will get a headache. 5. When the mango season arrives there will be joy in every heart, because this fruit is sweet and juicy. 6. On hearing her voice I laughed as I ran towards her. 7. Lucknow is worth seeing. 8. That small boy will not be fit for this task. 9. Do the work according to my order. 10. The criminal will get punishment according to the law. 11. I will place this cheque in your charge ; cash it when you please. 12. In connection with this allegation let me say something. 13. The witness is reliable in my view.

LESSON XXVIII

DUPLICATION OF WORDS

The duplication of words is frequent, (a) by repetition of the same word, or (b) by addition of a synonym or word approximating in meaning, or (c) of a rhyming or jingling word without meaning. In the case of the verb only the participles are duplicated. Duplication gives an idea of extension or distribution over time or space.

(*a*) (1) Noun, singular : bar bar, *time and again* ; kona kona, *every corner* ; səf səf, *in ranks* ; des des ke raja, *rajas of different countries* ; səɽək səɽək, *all the way along* ; kynare kynare, *all along the bank* ; admi admi meŋ fərq hota həy, *all men are different*.

Noun, plural : batoŋ batoŋ meŋ, *in the course of conversation* ; ratoŋ rat, *the night long*.

(2) Adjective, singular : thoɽa thoɽa mylkər bəwht hojata həy, *a little at a time becomes much* ; ʈhəndi ʈhəndi həva cəl rəhi həy, *a nice cool breeze is blowing* ; adhi adhi rat tək, *even till midnight*.

Adjective, plural : bəɽe bəɽe dərəxt, *many big trees* ; hathi ke kya ləmbe ləmbe daŋt həyŋ, *what long tusks the elephant has!* uŋt ki bhari bhari pəlkeŋ həyŋ, *the eyelids of the camel are heavy* ; həm logoŋ ko əpni əpni jəgəh pər rəyhna cahie, *we must stay each in his own place*.

(3) Interrogative pronoun : kəwn kəwn aega (aeŋge), *what various persons will come ?* ys sənduq meŋ kya kya cizeŋ həyŋ, *what various things are there in this box ?*

(4) Participle : əwrət pəkate pəkate bylkwl thək gəi, *the woman got utterly tired cooking* ; məyŋ mərte mərte bəc gəya, *I just escaped death* ; səvar gyrte gyrte bəc gəya, *the rider just escaped falling* ; swn swnkər, *by continuing to listen* ; rəyh rəyh kər, *continuing but interruptedly* ; ws ne gədhe ko mar markər cəlaya, *he made the ass go by continuous beatings*.

(5) Postposition : voh ws ke piche piche dəwɽa, *he ran close behind him* ; goli mere syr ke upər upər nykəl gəi, *the bullet went past close above my head*.

(6) Adverb : ʈhik ʈhik bətao, *state exactly*.

(7) Cardinal numbers : do do rupəe, *two rupees each* ; voh do do kərke əndər aeŋge, *they will enter two at a time* ; məyŋ ne yeh cizeŋ saɽhe sat sat rupəe ko mol liŋ, *I bought these articles for seven and a half rupees each*.

N.B.—The following expressions should be noted : **koi koi,** *a few* ; **koi na koi,** *someone or other* ; **kwch kwch,** *a little* ; **kwch na kwch,** *something or other* ; **ghər ka ghər,** *the whole house* ; **səb ke səb,** *one and all* ; **an ki an meŋ,** *in a trice* ; **salha sal,** *many years* (ha, class. Pers. pl. of inanimate nouns) ; **əvvəl hi əvvəl,** *in the first place* ; **dyl hi dyl meŋ,** *down in one's heart, silently to oneself* ; **hathoŋ hath,** *hand over hand, quickly* ; **wn ke bicoŋ bic,** *in their very midst* ; **bəna bənaya,** *ready-made* ; **ləda lədaya,** *ready-laden* ; **swni swnai bat,** *hearsay* ; **than pər than kəpɽa,** *bale on bale of cloth* ; **saət bəsaət,** *hour by hour* ; **dər dər, dər bədər,** *at every door, from door to door* ; **kəm se kəm,** *at least* ; **zyada se zyada,** *at most.*

(*b*) Synonym or word approximating in meaning :

(1) Noun : **nəwkər cakər,** *servants* ; **taun bəwht zor ʃor se phəyla,** *the plague spread with virulence* ; **ɣwl ʃor məcana,** *to make a din* ; **pwlys ne ws ke bəyanat ki chan bin ki,** *the police investigated* (*sift* ; *see*) *his statements.*

(2) Adjective : **məyle kwcəyle kəpɽe,** *dirty clothes* ; **saf swthre kəpɽe,** *nice and clean clothes* ; **həra bhəra,** *verdant.*

(3) Verb : **soc səməjhkər,** *after well considering* ; **jan bujhkər,** *knowingly.*

(*c*) A rhyming or jingling word without meaning, formed by substituting **v** for the initial letter of the noun : **kaɣəz vaɣəz,** *the various papers* ; **yeh log həmeʃa ələg rəyhte həyŋ, kəbhi xəlt məlt nəhiŋ hote,** *these persons always keep aloof, they never mix.*

Vocabulary

ka **bhəgoɽa,** fugitive
ka **qəsd,** purpose
ka **karobar,** business
ka **len den,** trading
ka **bij,** seed
ki **geŋd,** ball
ki **ʃerarət,** mischief
ki **dyanətdari,** honesty

pəkəɽna, to capture
aŋkh bəcana, to escape observation
reŋgna, riŋgna, to creep, crawl
bona, to sow
ghurna, to gaze
thək jana, to get tired

Examples

uŋʈ bin pani kəi kəi dyn gwzar deta həy.	The camel can go several days without water.
ɖənɖa marne vale ne zor se mara lekyn var xali gəya.	The batter hit out vigorously, but missed his stroke.
koi na koi nəwkər jagta (bedar) hoga.	Some servant or other must be awake.
ys kytab ke nəe chape hathoŋ hath xətm hogəe.	The new editions of this book were quickly exhausted.
mwjhe ws se jan pəyhcan nəhiŋ.	I am not acquainted with him.
yeh syrf jan pəyhcan ka admi həy.	This person is only an acquaintance.
admioŋ ki bhiʈ ki bhiʈ ja rəhi thi.	The people were going along in crowds.
yuswf nam ek ʃəxs tez dəwɽne se kaŋpte kaŋpte bahər besəbri se ap ka yntyzar kər rəha həy.	A man named Joseph, trembling through running fast, awaits you outside impatiently.
ys kytab meŋ ws ne syrf əyse vaqyat lykhe jo ws pər gwzre.	In this book he has written only such incidents as befell him.
mwlaqat ke rəsmi əlfaz kəyhte kəyhte ws ne mez se ʈhokər khai.	While repeating the customary words of salutation on meeting he stumbled against the table.

Exercise XXVIII

1. I told him as many as ten times. 2. For many years he and I did not meet. 3. The ball passed just overhead. 4. Keeping up with the fugitive he at length captured him. 5. Knowingly and purposely he did this mischief. 6. Let us take a walk by the river, keeping along the bank till we reach the field where the schoolboys will be playing cricket. 7. The club-servants are like a small regiment. 8. On the table heaps of papers were lying. 9. Creeping on and on they entered the enemy's line unnoticed. 10. His honesty in business and trading was well

known. 11. He was laughing as he sang the song. 12. I watched the sower sowing his seed. 13. I gazed and gazed till my eyes grew tired.

LESSON XXIX

ARABIC AND PERSIAN WORDS AND PHRASES

In Urdu literature words and phrases from Arabic and Persian abound. Many of the words have long since gained currency and an established place in the **rozmərra** or Hindustani as it is now spoken. Phrases are generally less capable of naturalisation, but the following are some of many in frequent use :

(*a*) **kəm o beʃ**, *more or less* ; **asman o zəmin ka fərq**, *the difference between heaven and earth* ; **mwlk ki xydmət ke lie voh jan o mal se isar kia**, *for the service of his country he made sacrifice with life and property.*

N.B.—" **o** " is " *and* " in this Persian formation ; neither noun should be a Hindi word.

(*b*) **zəmin-e zərxez**, *a rich soil* ; **mwlk-e iran**, *the country of Iran*; **cəʃm-e bəd dur**, *the evil eye be far off!*

N.B.—In this Persian combination of a noun and its following adjective or of two nouns in a possessive relationship, the bond of connection is indicated by **yzafət**, the short vowel between them ; it should not be used in combination with a Hindi word : **gənga dərya**, *the river Ganges.*

(*c*) Expressions frequently heard are : **ynʃalla(h)**, *if God will* ; **maʃalla(h)**, *God forbid!* (Arabic : *what God wills*) ; **təwba**, *repentance, horrible! good gracious!* **la həwl**, an abbreviation of a Quranic sentence : " *There is no power or strength except in God!* "—an expression used at sight or sound of anything disagreeable ; the expression known as the **təkbir** or magnification : **əllahu əkbər**, *God is great!* **bysmylla(h)**, *in* or *with the name of God*—an expression used at the commencement of an act or task, e.g. eating, sacrificing ; **nəmək-həlal**, *loyal, faithful to one's salt*; **nəmək-həram**, *disloyal, unfaithful to one's salt.*

(*d*) The Persian comparative degree is represented by the word **behtər**, *better* : **behtər, yeh kijie**, *very good, do so, Sir!* **yeh təjviz kəhiŋ behtər həy**, *this proposal is far better* ; **yeh səb se behtər həy**, *this is better than all* ; and by **mehtər**, *greater, prince* (a term still applied to one ruling house, but also applied as a complimentary designation to sweepers). The superlative **behtərin** is used : **behtərin təriqa yeh həy**, *the best method is this.*

(*e*) Prepositional phrases : **bənysbət**, *in relation to* ; **bənysbət ys ke, ys ki bənysbət,** *compared with this* ; **bəɣəyr,** *without* ; **bəɣəyr khane ke** or **khae bəɣəyr,** *without eating* ; **roz bəroz,** *day by day* ; **saət bəsaət,** *hour by hour, moment by moment.*

N.B.—**ɣəyr** is frequent in such expressions as : **ɣəyr mərd,** *stranger* ; **ɣəyr mwlki,** *foreigner* ; **vəɣəyra,** *et cetera.*

(*f*) The following are often used as prefixes, **ba** (*with*), **be** (*without*), **bəd** (*bad*), **kəm** (*deficient*), **la** and **na** (*not*) : **baədəb,** *polite* ; **baiman,** *faithful* ; **baqayda,** *regular, according to rule* ; **beədəb,** *rude* ; **becara,** *helpless* ; **beiman,** *faithless* ; **bemysal, benəzir,** *unequalled* ; **beqayda,** *irregular* ; **bədbəxt,** *unlucky* ; **bəddyanət,** *dishonest* ; **bədnəsib,** *unfortunate* ; **bədsurət,** *ugly* ; **kəmbəxt,** *unlucky* ; **kəmxərc,** *thrifty* ; **kəmzor,** *weak* ; **lacar,** *helpless* ; **lapərva,** *careless* ; **nawmed,** *hopeless* ; **naraz,** *displeased* ; **nadan,** *ignorant* ; **naynsaf,** *unjust.*

N.B.—**be, bəɣəyr,** and the Hindi **byna** or **byn,** all meaning "*without,*" may be used with (i) nouns, or (ii) verbs ; **be** always precedes, the others sometimes follow :

(i) **beʃəkk,** *without doubt* ; **becara,** *without resource* ; **byn pani,** *without water* ; **bəɣəyr hwkm (ke), hwkm ke bəɣəyr,** *without an order.*

(ii) (1) With the singular masculine inflected past participle : **be mere kəhe (hue),** *without my telling* ; **byn soce, soce byna,** *without thinking* ; **khae bəɣəyr,** *without eating.* (2) Sometimes with the infinitive and **ke** : **bəɣəyr khane ke,** *without eating.*

(*g*) Adverbial phrases : **fəwrən,** *immediately* ; **yttyfaqən (yttyfaq se),** *by chance* ; **zahyrən (zahyra),** *obviously* ; **mejburən,** *perforce.* Also the Persian imperatives : **xa(h) məxa(h)** (*wish, don't wish*), *willy-nilly.*

D *

Vocabulary

ka əjayb-xana, museum
ka yhata, compound
ka pəsina, perspiration
ka ʃəyhtir, joist
ki taqət, strength
ki peʃani, forehead

ki zəmanasazi, sycophancy
kyfayətʃyar, thrifty
bevəfa, disloyal
yəksaŋ, alike, equally
daxyl hona, to enter
poŋchna, to wipe

Examples

məyŋ ap ka məʃkur o məmnun huŋ.

I am grateful and obliged to you.

dəwɽte dəwɽte voh bedəm ho-gəya, məgər thoɽi der aram lekər taza dəm phyr cəl dia.

He was out of breath from running, but after resting a short time he set off again fresh.

kəhaŋ məyŋ kəhaŋ ap—mere əwr ap ke kəmal o hwnər meŋ zəmin o asman ka fərq həy.

How can I compare with you ? There's a world of difference in our accomplishments.

bənysbət ys choțe kəmre ke ap ka kəmra vəsi həy.

In proportion to this small room yours is spacious.

bəyəyr kaləɽya gwlubənd pəyhne voh ədalət-e alya ke ehate məŋ daxyl hua.

Without collar or scarf he entered the compound of the High Court.

bəyəyr ɣəwr əwr fykr ke ws ne əysi bevəqufi ki.

Without thought or care he committed such folly.

Exercise XXIX

1. Between the miserly and the thrifty there is a world of difference. 2. Day by day a child's strength increases. 3. Without permission one cannot enter the museum, or even its compound. 4. He arrived breathless and hatless, and wiping the perspiration from his forehead. 5. There are two dozen pencils more or less in this box. 6. He is a disloyal, unjust and dishonest man ; who could be so foolish as to trust his word ?

7. Honesty is a better policy than sycophancy. 8. Persia (mwlk-e fars) is nowadays called Iran, and its inhabitants Iranis. 9. The sun shines on rich and poor equally. 10. At most this joist is twenty feet long, and perhaps is a little less. 11. He did this under compulsion.

MISCELLANEOUS

CALENDAR

THE year (bərəs ; sal) is solar among the Hindus, lunar among the Muslims. In either case it is divided into twelve months (məhina). European names for the months are freely used ; they are masculine in gender, but məy and the three ending in i are treated by some as feminine :

jənvəri,	January	jwlai ; jəwlai,	July
fərvəri,	February	əgəst,	August
marc,	March	sytəmbər,	September
əprəyl,	April	əktubər,	October
məy,	May	nəvəmbər,	November
jun,	June	dəsəmbər,	December

For the days of the week (həfte ke dyn) the following nouns are in common use :

ytvar,	Sunday	jwmerat,	Thursday
pir ; somvar,	Monday	jwma,	Friday
məngəl,	Tuesday	sənicər,	Saturday
bwddh,	Wednesday		

CARDINAL POINTS OF THE COMPASS

	Hindi	*Urdu*
North,	wttər	ʃymal
South,	dəkkhyn	jənub
East,	purəb	məʃryq
West,	pəcchym	məɣryb

N.B.—(a) all are masculine in gender ;

(b) hyndostan ki ʃymal məɣrybi sərhəd, *the N.W. frontier of India.*

OFFICE

1. məyŋ kəl se roz dəftər jauŋga.
2. mera cəprasi ghər pər zəruri kaɣəzat lekər aya.
3. kya kwch xəttoŋ pər dəstxətt kərne baqi həyŋ ?
4. mwjhe fwlaŋ fwlaŋ ki fayl do.
5. yeh zəruri kaɣəzoŋ meŋ nəthi kər do.
6. ryjystər kəhaŋ həy ?
7. mez qələm dəvat vəɣəyra saf rəkha kəro.
8. syahi-cus dykhai nəhiŋ deta.
9. məyŋ ʃamko kanfərəŋs (jəlse) meŋ huŋga.
10. yeh xətt meri prayvət fayl meŋ ləga do.

TRAVELLING

1. məyŋ səməndər ke raste yurəp janevala huŋ.
2. mwjhe kyʃti ka səfər bəɽa pəsənd həy.
3. swna həy ky həvai jəhaz həfte meŋ tin dəfa vylayət ko jate
   həyn—wn həvai jəhazoŋ meŋ kəi həvai kyʃtiaŋ bhi həyŋ.
4. hyndostan meŋ rel-gaɽi ka səfər mwjhe nəhiŋ bhata.
5. vylayət meŋ rel-gaɽi ke əmumən do dəbbe (dərje) hote həyŋ—
   pəyhla əwr tisra—kysi kysi rel meŋ dusra.
6. hyndostan meŋ rel-gaɽi ke car dəbbe (dərje) hote həyŋ—pəyhla
   dusra deɽha əwr tisra.
7. kəi dynoŋ ke səfər ke bad məyŋ thəkavət se mər rəha tha.
8. yəhaŋ se vylayət motər-gaɽi pər jane meŋ kytne dyn ləgeŋge ?
9. həvai jəhaz se kəraci se ləndən tin dyn ka rasta həy.

RADIO

1. Swna gəya həy ky əb motər-gaɽi meŋ bhi redyo ləgaya jata
   həy.
2. məyŋ əbhi pən-byjli ghər se aya huŋ.
3. byjli meŋ taqət bəwht hoti həy.
4. redyo steʃən byjli hi ki bədəwlət brəwdkast kərta həy.
5. məyŋ kəl ynglystan ke vəzir-e azəm ki təqrir zərur redyo se
   swnuŋga.

6. əgəst ko kangrəs ka yjlas honevala həy.
7. səb syasi moaməlat pər bəyhs ki jaegi.
8. byjli bətti bwjha do.
9. ws ka bətən kəhaŋ həy ?
10. meri mezvali bətti (ţebyl ləymp) ka bətən wsi ke sath həy.
11. chətvali byjli bəttioŋ ka bətən əmumən divar pər hota həy.
12. bəyţrivale redyo sət ki zyada taqət nəhiŋ hoti.
13. mwjhe to aţh bəlb ka redyo sət pəsənd həy.

VOCABULARY

cəprasi, office messenger
dəstxətt, signature
nəthi, thread for file, file
dəvat, inkstand
syahi-cus, blotting-paper
bhata, pleasing
əmumən, generally
dəbba, class
dərja, class, degree

thəkavət, weariness
pən byjli ghər, hydro-electric
    station
bədəwlət, by means of
vəzir-e azəm, Prime Minister
təqrir, speech
syasi, political
bəyhs, discussion

TELEPHONE

myrza sahyb. əre yeh ţelifun ki ghənţi bəj rəhi həy—dekho to kəwn həy.

nəwkər. ji sahb . . . myrza mohəmməd əli ki koţhi—ji-ji—bəwht əccha sahb—əbhi ek mynəţ meŋ.

myrza. kəwn həy.

nəwkər. tahyr sahb ki avaz malum hoti həy.

myrza. əccha lao ydhər—myrza moho . . .

tahyr. kəhie jənab—məyŋ ne soca ky myrza sahb ko yttyla de duŋ ky məyŋ kəlkətte se zynda vapəs ləwţ aya.

myrza. kəho miaŋ tahyr—bhəi mana ky twm kəlkətte se ho-ae—əb ys ka mətləb yeh to nəhiŋ ky dostoŋ ko bhwla bəyţho.

tahyr. kya ərz kəruŋ—kəi dəfa ane ka yrada kia lekyn . . .

myrza. lekyn kya—əme twm to həva meŋ cəlte ho həva meŋ—axyr yeh bhi kya—kəho chwţţiaŋ kəyse gwzriŋ.

tahyr. kya ərz kəruŋ—kya kəyhne kəlkətte ke—bəs hyndostan ki vəlayət səməjh lo—syvae zəmindoz gaṛi ke baqi səb kwch məwjud həy.

myrza. bhai həm to dehati ʈhəyre—zəra ʈhik ʈhik bətao.

tahyr. əccha pəl bhər ʈhəyro məyŋ sygrəʈ jəla luŋ.

myrza (nəwkər se). əre miaŋ chəbbən—hwqqa yəhaŋ leao.

tahyr. haŋ to—məyŋ yeh kəyh rəha tha ky kəlkətte meŋ kya kya dekha—bhai mwjhe vəhaŋ ki ʈrəymeŋ bəwht pəsənd aiŋ—zəra bhər ʃor nəhiŋ hota—dylli ki tərəh nəhiŋ ky ghənʈi bəjane ki zərurət ho—log ʃor swnkər xwd hi rasta saf kər dete həyŋ—ji nəhiŋ—vəhaŋ ʈrəymeŋ bəwht tezi əwr xamoʃi se cəlti həyŋ—dərja əvvəl meŋ to pənkhe bhi ləge hwe həyŋ.

myrza. byjli ke pənkhe ?

tahyr. ji haŋ—byjli ke—bəs dyl cahta həy ky sara dyn ysi meŋ bəyʈhe bəyʈhe gwzər jae—haŋ yeh to kəyhna bhul hi gəya —vəhaŋ məyŋ ne ʈrəwli bəseŋ bhi dekhiŋ.

myrza. wn meŋ bhi pənkhe the kya.

tahyr. bhai twm to ɣəzəb kərte ho—əb hər jəgəh pənkhe thoṛe hi ləgae jate həyŋ.

myrza. əgər ʈrəwli bəs bhi byjli se cəlti həy to ws meŋ pənkhe kyoŋ nəhiŋ ləgae jate.

tahyr. twm to əysi bateŋ kərte ho jəyse məyŋ kəlkətte ke byjli ghər ka malyk huŋ—əgər mere zymme hota to məyŋ to dərəxtoŋ ko bhi pənkhe ləga deta.

myrza. kya kəyhne həyŋ apke—əmeŋ yəhaŋ ao to bateŋ hoŋ.

tahyr. bhai zəra ʈelifun pəkṛe rəhiega—kysi ne bahər ki ghənʈi bəjai . . . o ho—lətif sahyb həyŋ—aie sahb təʃrif laie.

lətif. ʈelifun to ap ne ləgva lia—əb ysi ko hath meŋ pəkṛe bəyʈhe rəyhte həyŋ.

tahyr. məyŋ myrza sahyb se bateŋ kər rəha tha.

lətif. kəwn—mohəmməd ali se—lao zəra məyŋ bhi adab kəyh duŋ—bhəi mwjhe to ys bəla se ḍər ləgta həy—hwqqe ki avaz a rəhi həy—(uŋci) kəhie myrza sahb myzaj əcche həyŋ.

myrza. kəwn lətif—bhai yuŋ ʈhik nəhiŋ—tahyr ko lekər yəhaŋ cəle ao to bateŋ hoŋ.

lətif.   tahyr kəyhte həyŋ ky kəl səhi.

myrza.   tahyr to kəlkətte ki xabeŋ dekh rəha həy—kəl se mere haŋ bəwht am ae hwe həyŋ—əgər cəle ao to hyssa myl jaega.

lətif.   to həm zərur ate həyŋ—koi adh ghənṭa ləgega.

myrza.   kəlkətte ki ṭrəym gaṛi hoti to ʃayəd paŋc hi mynəṭ ləgte.

Notes

əre ! *O you!* interjection used in addressing an inferior ; əme(ŋ), in addressing a friend, etc.
koṭhi, *a firm, dwelling.*

yttyla, *information.*

mana (past participle of **manna**), *admitted, granted.*

mətləb, *meaning ; " this does not mean that you should forget your friends."*

ərz kərna, *to represent, state humbly.*

yrada, *intention.*

həva meŋ, *" you are up in the clouds."*

kya kəyhne, *" what can one say about C. ?—you could consider it the occident in India."*

zəmindoz, *underground.*

dehati ṭhəyre, *" merely villagers "* ; ṭhəyrna, *to tarry ; be proved, established.*

pəl, *eyelid, moment* ; pəl bhər, *just a moment.*

jəlana, *to light.*

xamoʃi, *silence.*

dərja əvvəl, *first class.*

pənkha, *fan.*

ɣəzəb, *anger* ; ɣəzəb ki qəhətsali, *a terrible famine* ; ɣəzəb kərte ho, *" you are expecting too much."*

zymma, *responsibility.*

adab kəyhna, *to pay respects.*

bəla, *trial, calamity* : *" I am afraid of this wretched thing (i.e. the phone)."*

xab dekhna, *to dream.*

VOCABULARY

(The numerals refer to Lessons in which the word occurs or its use is exemplified.)

A

a.m.	swbəh 26
able	qabyl 18; layq 27
to be —	səkna 14
about	təqribən 25; qərib 27 ; koi 24
about to	cahna 13
above	upər 27
abundance	kəsrət 25
abuse	gali ; gali dena 13
abused, be	gali khana 16
accept	qəbul kərna 18
accident	hadysa 18
accompany	sath dena 9; holena 16
accomplishments	hwnər o kəmal 29
accordance, in	mwafyq 27
account	hysab 18
on — of	mare 17, 27 ; bays, səbəb, vəjəh 27
accusation	ylzam 27
accused	mwdda ələy 20
accustomed	adi hona 9
acquaintance	jan pəyhcan 28
action	hərkət 13; əml 21
adjust	dwrwst kərna 9
adopt	mwtəbənna kərna 16
adopted	mwŋh bola 15
advance	peʃgi 20
to —	bəɽhna 14

advertise	yʃtehar kərna 27
advice	səlah 27
affair	bat 5; moamla 24
affection	pyar 10
after	bad, piche 27
afterwards	bad meŋ 8; piche 27
again	phyr 7
against	xylaf 27
age	wmr 27
aged	syn-rəsida 27
air	həva 15
aircraft-carrier	təiyara bərdar jəhaz 21
airing	həva khana 9
alien	pərdesi 21
alight	wtərna 14
alike	yəksaŋ 22, 29
all	səb 3
allegation	ylzam 27
allow	dena 11
allowed, be	pana 11
alms	bhik 8
alongside	bərabər 27
along with	ke sath, ke həmra(h) 15, 27
already	pəyhle (hi se) 27
also	bhi 5
although	əgərcy, bavwjudeky 7 ; go 22
always	həmeʃa 8; bərabər 27
amends	təlafi kərna 18

amulet	taviz 1	*at least*	kəm se kəm 11
ancient	pwrana 4	— *most*	zyada se zyada 28
anger	ɣwssa 19		
angry	ɣwsse hona 7; xəfa hona 12; bygəɽna 18	— *once*	fəwrən 9
		attack	həmla kərna 17
		attention	təvəjjoh 1, 19
animal	janvər 5; həyvan 22	*await*	yntyzar kərna 28
		awake	bedar 28
anna	ana 25	*to* —	jagna (intr.) 19; jəgana (tr.) 19
annoyed	bezar 17		
annual	salana 18	*axe*	kwlhaɽi 15
any	kwch 3		
anyone	koi 3		
apologise	mwafi maŋgna 17	**B**	
appear	nəzər ana 9; dykhai dena 9,11	*back* (adv.)	vapəs 7, 12
		bad	bwra 2; xərab 3; ʃərir 16
appearance	surət 22		
apple	seb 20	*baggage*	saman, əsbab 12
application	dərxast 27	*bale*	than 28
apply	ləgana 11	*ball*	geŋd 28
appointment	yqrar 21	*bandit*	ḍaku 17
approve	mənzur kərna 18	*bank* (pavement)	kynara 28
area	rəqba 25		
argue	bəyhs kərna 17	*Bank*	bəynk 18
arithmetic	hysab 18	*bare*	nənga 20, 27
arm	bazu 8	*basket*	ṭokri 25
army	fəwj 8	*bat*	ḍənḍa 28
around	yrd gyrd 27	*battle*	ləɽai 8
arrayed	arasta 21	*be*	hona 4
arrive	pəwhŋcna 7	*bear*	rich 17
art (craft)	hwnər 10	*beat*	marna, piṭna 12, 16
artless	sada-myzaj 18		
ashtray	rakhdan 25	*beaten*	pyṭna, mar khana 16
ask	puchna 11		
— *for*	maŋgna 8	*beautiful*	xubsurət 4
assure	yəqin dylana 11	*because*	cuŋky, kyoŋky 27
at	pər 1		
— *house of*	haŋ 27	— *of*	ke mare 11, 27
— *last*	axyr ko (kar) 14, 15	*become*	bənna 19
		bed	pələng, bystər 17

bedroom	sone ka kəmra 11	*blood*	xun 15
befall	pəṛna 17; gwzərna 28	*blow, give*	thəppəṛ marna 18
before, ago	pəyhle, peſtər 27	*blue*	nila 21
begin	ləgna 11 ; ſwru kərna 14	*board*	təxta 11
		boast	ḍiŋ marna 18
beginning	ſwru, ybtyda, əvvəl 14	*boat*	kyſti 17
		body	bədən 8
behave towards	swluk (bərtao) kərna 18; peſ ana 18	*boil*	phwṭna, wbəlna (intr.) 19; wbalna (tr.) 9
behind	piche 27, 28	*bomber*	bəmbar 11;
belch	ḍəkar 9	*— plane*	bəmbar həvai jəhaz 21
believe	yəqin kərna 18; manna 15	*book*	kytab 3
bell	ghənṭa, ghənṭi 8	*bookcase*	kwtwb əlmari 4
below	nice, təle 17	*boon*	ɣənimət 21
belt	peṭi 15	*bottle*	botəl 23
bend (road)	moṛ 8	*box*	bəks 9; sənduq 19
bend	jhwkna (intr.), jhwkana (tr.) 18	*boy*	ləṛka 1
		brain	dymaɣ 11
beneath	nice, təle 17	*branch*	ḍali 12; ṭəyhni 21
benefit	fayda 12		
Bengal	bəngal 18	*brass*	pitəl 3
beside	pas 27	*brave*	bəhadwr 7; dyler 24
— oneself	ape se bahər 20		
besides	əlava 27	*bravery*	bəhadwri 8
best	behtərin 29	*bread*	roṭi 9
bet	ſərt 10	*break*	toṛna 19, 21
better	behtər 12, 29	*breakfast*	naſta, hazri 20
big	bəṛa 2	*breath*	dəm 7, 21; saŋs 12
bigha	bigha, bygha 21		
bind	bəṇdhna 15	*breathless*	bedəm 21, 29
bird (small)	cyṛia 1	*breeze*	həva 27; nəsim 15
bird (general)	pərynd 17, 20		
birthday	salgyrəh 21	*bride*	dwlhən 18
bite	kaṭna 7	*bridegroom*	dwlha 18
black	kala 3	*bridge*	pwl 27
blanket	kəmbəl 21	*brief*	mwxtəsər 27
blind	əndha 3	*brightness*	rəwſni 22

bring	lana 2, 9	*camel*	uŋṭ 28
broad	cəwṛa 2	*canal*	nəyhr 12
broken, be	ṭuṭna 9, 19	*candle*	mombətti 9
get —	ṭuṭ jana 16	*caned, be*	bed khana 16
brother	bhai 1	*cantonment*	chaoni 25
brother-in-law	bəyhnoi 21	*capture*	pəkəṛna 28; qəyd
brow	teori 17; peʃani		kərna 18
	29	*care*	fykr 29
brown	bhura 15	*careful*	xəbərdar 5
build	bənana 25	*carefree, care-*	lapərva, 15, 29
building	məkan 7	*less*	
bull	saŋḍ 18	*carelessness*	lapərvai 16
bullock	bəyl 18	*carpenter*	bəṛhəi 1
bullock-cart	chəkṛa, bəylgaṛi	*carriage*	gaṛi 10
	20	*closed* —	bəndgaṛi 25
bullet	goli 11	*railway* —	relgaṛi 6
burrow	byl 23	*carry away*	lejana 6
burst	phəṭna (intr.)15,	— *out*	tamil kərna 18
	19; phaṛna (tr.)	*cartridge*	kartus 16
	19	*cash*	nəqd 18; nəqdi
business	lenden 9; karo-		21
	bar 28	*to* —	toṛna 18
but	məgər, lekyn 2	*casket*	ḍybbi 3
butter	məkkhən 10 ;	*cat*	bylli 1
	ghi 1	*catch*	pəkəṛna 11
buy	lena 12; xəridna	*cauliflower*	phulgobhi 19
	25; molna 25	*cause*	səbəb 16
		cautious	xəbərdar 5
		cavalry	rysala 8
	C	*central*	bicvala 26
		centre	bic 26
cabbage	gobhi 19	*century*	sədi 14
calamity	bəla 21; mwsibət	*ceremony*	təqrib 18
	24	*certainly*	zərur 5
Calcutta	kəlkətta 1	*certainty*	yəqin 5
call	bwlana 9;	*chair*	kwrsi 7; cəwki
	pwkarna 12		22
— *out*	avaz dena 10	*chance*	yttyfaq 27
called, be	kəyhlana 16	*by* —	yttyfaqən 27
— (*meeting*)	mwnaqyd hona	*change* (*money*)	rezgi 18
	16	*charge, in*	həvale 27

charming	dylcəsp 9	*common*	am, mwʃtəryk 24
cheap	səsta 25	*companion*	sathi 1
cheque	cyk 18	*compare*	mylana 21
chief	sərdar 18	*compared*	bənysbət 27;·
child	bəcca 19;	*with*	kəhaŋ 29
	(pl.), bal bəcce	*compel*	məjbur kərna 13
	20, əwlad 21	*compelled, be*	məjbur hona 13
childhood	bəcpən 6	*completely*	bylkwl, saf, ek
chill	sərdi 11		dəm 21
Christian	isvi 27	*compose*	təsnif kərna 18
church	gyrja 8	*compound*	ehata 1
cigarette	sygrət 19	*compulsorily*	məjburən 13
cigarette-box	sygrətdan 10	*conclusion*	xatyma 14
city	ʃəyhr 7	*conduct*	cal cələn 20
claim	daⱱa kərna 18	*congratulate*	mwbarəkbad
clean	saf 6; saf swthra		dena 5
	28	*congregational*	jame 26
clearly	saf, xub 11	*connection, in*	ke bare meŋ, ki
cleave to	ləgna 11		babət 11; mwtə-
clerk	babu 27		əllyq 27
climate	ab o həva 20	*consider*	səməjhna 10;
climb	cəɽhna 15		socna 28
closed	bənd 9	*consideration*	lehaz 24 ; xəyal
cloth	kəpɽa, 6, 28		20
cloud	badəl 8	*console*	təsəlli dena (dy-
coat	koṭ 15		lana) 11
cobbler	moci 6	*consult*	məʃⱱərəh (səlah)
coffee	qəyhva 2		kərna 18
cold	sərdi 5	*contained, be*	səmana 15
— *(in head)*	zwkam 11	*contend*	ləɽna 16
— *(adj.)*	ṭhənḍa 7	*contentment*	rəzaməndi,
— *season*	sərdi (sərdioŋ)		qənaət 21
	ka məwsəm 12	*control*	zəbt kərna 12
collar	kaləɽ 29	*converse*	bat cit
collect	jəma kərna 18		(gwftəgu) kərna
colour	rəng 15		18, 21
comb	kənghi kərna 22	*converted*	iman lana 9
come	ana 7, 9	*cook*	bavərci 6
— *out*	nykəlna 7	*to* —	pəkana 6
comfort	təsəlli dena 19	*cool*	ṭhənḍa 7
commence	ʃwru kərna 14	*coolie*	qwli 6

copy	nəql kərna 17	
— *book*	kapi 13	
cork	kag, kak 26	
corner	kona 28	
— *of road*	moɽ 8	
correct	dwrwst 20	
corresponding *to*	mwtabyq 27	
cough	khaŋsna 11	
country	mwlk, des, deʃ 5	
native —	vətən 20	
courage, lose	hymmət harna 21	
course, in	dəwran (əsna) meŋ 27	
court	dərbar 11	
law-court	ədalətgah 20	
cow	gae 6	
cowardly	bwzdyl 24	
crawl, creep	reŋgna, riŋgna 28	
criminal	mwjrym 27	
professional *criminal*	jəraym peʃa admi 27	
crooked	teɽha	
crop	fəsl 25	
crossroads	cəwrasta, cəwraha 21	
crowd	bhiɽ 28	
cruel	berəyhm 11	
curd	dəhi 1	
currant	kyʃmyʃ 26	
current lan-guage	rozmərra 29	
curtain	pərda 9	
customary	rəsmi 28	
cut	katna 7	
be —	kətna, kət jana 15	
cute	calak 22	

D

dagger	xənjər 20
daily	roz, hər roz 9 ; rozana (adj.) 27
dainty	barik 10
dam	bənd 18
damage	nwqsan 19
danger	xətra 16, 24
dark	əndhera (n., adj.) 6, 9
darn	rəfu kərna 9
date	tarix 16
daughter	beti 21
dawn	fəjr 9
day	dyn 1 ; roz 9
daylight	dhup 9
deaf	bəyhra 16
deal with	səməjhna 21
dear	qiməti, məy-hŋga 25
death	məwt 15
debt	qərz 9
decay	sətna 11
deceived, be	dhokha khana 16
decision	fəysla 27
deep	gəyhra 8
defame	bədnami kərna 18
defeated, be	ʃykəst khana 16
deficient	kəm 13
delay	der 9
delicate	nazwk 10
deny	ynkar kərna 9, 27
departure	rəvangi 27
deprived	məyhrum, 16, 19
depth	gəyhrai 18
descend	wtərna 14
desert	səhra 1

deserving of	mwstəhyq 27	*draw*	kheŋcna, khiŋc-
desire	cahna 7, 13		na 19
desolate	swnsan 11	*— curtain*	pərda ḍalna 9
despairing	mayus 5	*drawer*	draz 23
destroy	bərbad kərna 24	*drawing-room*	gol kəmra 21
devise	nykalna 27	*drawn, be*	khyŋcna 19
diamond	hira 10	*dressing down,*	mərəmmət
die	mərna 7; ynty-	*give*	kərna 21
	qal hona 27	*drink*	pina 7, 9
difference	fərq 28	*drive*	cəlana 14
difficult	mwʃkyl 5, 12	*drown*	ḍubna 15
diligent	mehnəti 4;	*dumb*	guŋga 16
	(adv.) dyl ləga-	*duster*	jhaʈən 17
	kər 11	*duty*	fərz 18
din	ɣwl ʃor 28	*do one's —*	fərz əda kərna 18
diploma	sənəd 21		
direction	tərəf 27		
dirty	məyla 28		E
disappear	ɣayb hona 7		
dishonest	bəddyanət 29	*ear*	kan 1
disloyal	bevəfa, nəmək-	*early*	səvere 9
	həram 29	*earth*	zəmin 1
dismiss	rwxsət kərna 18	*easy*	asan 12
displeased	naraz 29	*eat*	khana 7, 19
distance	fasla 7; dur 14	*edition*	chapa 28
distant	dur 7	*education*	talim 12
distracted	bədhəvas 15	*effort*	koʃyʃ 13
district	zyla 24; ylaqa 12	*elapse*	gwzərna 27
divide	təqsim kərna 18	*electric light*	byjli bətti 9
do	kərna 9; (caus.)	*electrician*	byjli mystri 9
	kərana 19	*elegant*	səjila 22
doctor	həkim 24;	*elephant*	hathi 1
	ḍakʈər	*embankment*	bənd 18
dog	kwtta 1	*embrace*	gəle ləgana 11
doll	gwʈia 1, 24	*emissary*	bheja 15
donkey	gədha 28	*end*	ynteha 14
door	dərvaza 1; dər 28	*bring life to*	kam təmam
— keeper	dərban 11	*an —*	kərna 15, 20
double	dwgna 25	*in the —*	axyr meŋ 8
down	nice 15	*enemy*	dwʃmən 1, 5
dozen	dərjən 25	*engage*	rəkhna 12

favour, do a	ynayət kərna 18; ynayət fərmana 20	*floor*	fərʃ 17
		flour	aṭa 6
fear	ḍər 7; həwl 29	*flow*	bəyhna 15
to —	ḍərna 7	*flower*	phul 15
feed	khylana 19	*flower-pot*	gwlabdan 27
feel	məyhsus kərna 14	*fly*	məkkhi 23
		to —	wṛna 17
feeling	jəzba 18	*fog*	kohra 17
female	mada 1	*folly*	bevəqufi 12
fever	bwxar 9	*fond of*	pəsənd kərna 6
field	khet 20	*food*	khana 6
fight	ləṛna 16	*foolish*	bevəquf 3
fighting	ləṛai 8	*foot*	paoŋ 9
figure	surət 22	*— (measure)*	fwṭ 25
final	yntehai 14	*footstep*	qədəm 25
find	pana 11	*for*	ke lie (vaste) 9
fine (of material)	barik 10	*forbid*	məna kərna
		force	zor 1; zəbər-dəsti 19
— (splendid)	wmda 9		
to —	jwrmana kərna 18	*forehead*	peʃani 29
		foreigner	əjnəbi, ɣəyr-mwlki 18
fine-looking	xubsurət 22		
finger	wngli 20	*forest*	jəngəl 12
finish	xətm kərna 11	*forget*	bhulna 5
finished, be	xətm hona, cwkna 14	*forgive*	mwaf kərna 16
		forgiveness	mwafi 9
fire	ag 11	*fork*	kaŋṭa 9
fireworks	atyʃbazi 19	*formalism*	təkəllwf 8
firm (business)	kəmpəni 27	*former*	pəyhla 25; pəyhle (adv.) 5
first	pəyhla 25; əvvəl 14		
		forward	age 11
fish	məchli 9	*foul*	gənda 12
fisherman	mahigir 6	*found*	məwjud 20
fist	mwṭṭhi 25	*fountain*	fəvvara 19
fit	qabyl 18; layq 27	*four-year-old*	carsala 27
to —	ṭhik ana 9	*fresh*	taza 2
flash, to	cəməkna 8	*friend*	dost 4
flatter	xwʃaməd kərna 18	*frightsome*	ḍəraona 22
		front, in	age 11; samne 27
flesh (meat)	goʃt 7	*frontier*	sərhəd 21

fruit	phəl 3	*gore, to*	siŋg marna 18
fruitless	befayda 12	*government*	sərkar 18
fugitive	bhəgoṛa 28	*grain*	dana
fulfil	əda kərna 18	*grandfather*	dada 1
full	bhəra hua 7, 15	*grasping*	lalci 25
		grass	ghas 6
		grateful	məʃkur 29
	G	*graze*	cərna 20
		greater	əkbər, mehtər 29
gambling	jua 21	*green*	həra, səbz 28
game	bazi 10	*grief*	rənj 20
Ganges	gənga 2, 29	*grieved*	yəm (əfsos)
garden	baɣ 1, 11; bəɣica 11		khana 16
		groom	sais 9
gate	phaṭək 11	*ground*	zəmin 2
gatekeeper	dərban 11	*guard*	pəyhra 8
gaze	ghurna 15	*guess*	əndaz 27
generally	əksər 5	*by* —	əndazən 27
generosity	səxavət 22	*gun*	top 21
generous	səxi 11		
get	mylna 11; hasyl kərna, pana 21		
			H
girl	ləṛki 1		
give	dena 1, 9; (caus.)	*habit*	adət 9
	dylana 11, 19	*habitation*	abadi 26
— *up*	dedena 12	*hair*	bal 1
gladly	xwʃi se 1	*half*	adha 1
glance	nəzər 9	*in* —	do ṭwkṛe 21
glass	ʃiʃa 22	*hand*	hath 1
glove	dəstana 15	*handful*	mwṭṭhi bhər 25
go	jana 1, 9	*happiness*	xwʃi 1
— *backwards*	həṭna 9	*happy*	xwʃ 5
— *by* (*judge*)	pər jana 9	*hard*	səxt 2
— *past*	gwzərna 17, 27	*hare*	xərgoʃ 25
let —	choṛna 19	*harm*	nwqsan 19; hərj 24
goat	bəkri 1		
God	xwda 1; əlla(h) 29	*harsh*	kərəxt 24
		haste, make	jəldi kərna 15
gong	ghənṭa 8	*hat*	ṭopi 3
good	əccha 2	*have*	ke pas hona 15, 21
goods	səwda 12		

head	sər, syr 1	*hour*	ghənʈa 8; ghəɽi
health	syhhət 20		26; saət 29
	myzaj, təbiət 20	*house*	ghər 1; məkan 7
healthy	təndrwst 8	*how*	kys tərəh, kyoŋ-
heap	ḍher 24		kər 27
heaped	ḍher ləgna 24	*humble*	xaksar 20
hear	swnna 6	*hunger*	bhukh 11
hearsay	swni swnai bat	*hungry*	bhukha 10
	28	*hunt*	ʃykar kərna
heart	dyl 5; kəleja 21		(khelna) 10
heat	gərmi 5	*hunter*	ʃykari 10
heavy	bhari 28	*husband*	ʃəwhər 13
help	mədəd dena		
	(kərna) 11, 18		
helpless	lacar, becara	**I**	
	29		
here	yəhaŋ 3	*idea*	xəyal 27
hide	chypna 24	*ignorant*	nadan 29
high	wŋca 2	*illiterate*	ənpəɽh 16
High Court	ədalət-e alya 29	*image*	murət 15
Hijra	hyjra 27	*imagine*	təsəvvwr kərna
Hindu	hyndu 18		18
Hindustani	hyndostani	*immediately*	fəwran 19
hockey	haki 16	*impatience*	besəbri 28
hold, get a	qabu pana 11	*impatient*	betab 17
hole	gəɽha 8; byl 23;	*important*	əhəmm 5
get a —	phwʈna 19	*impossible*	namwmkyn 12
home	ghər 1	*incident*	vaqya 27, 28
at —	ghər pər 1	*increase*	bəɽhna 17
honest	dyanətdar 28	*incumbent*	lazym, dərkar 13
honesty	dyanətdari 28	*infantry*	pyada pəlʈən 8
honey	ʃəyhd 23	*inform*	xəbər kərna
honour	yzzət kərna 16,		(dena) 18
	20	*information*	xəbər 12
hoof	swm 1	*ink*	rəwʃnai 22
hooligan	gwnḍa 12	*inkstand*	dəvat 10
hope	wm(m)ed 11	*innumerable*	əngyna
hopeless	nawmed 29	*inside*	bhitər 9; əndər
horse	ghoɽa 1		27
horse race	ghoɽ dəwɽ 26	*insist*	ysrar kərna 18
hot	gərm 2	*instead*	yvəz 27

leg	ṭaŋg 16; paoŋ 21	*loyal*	vəfadar 27; nəmək-həlal 29
leisure	fwrsət 2	*luggage*	saman 8
length	ləmbai	*lunge*	cəkkər dena 9
at —	axyr ko 8		
less	kəm 27		
lesson	səbəq 13	**M**	
lest	kəhiŋ 5		
letter	cyṭṭhi 8; xətt 14	*Madam*	memsahb 20
lettering	hərf 15	*made, be*	bənna 19
level	bərabər, həmvar 26;	*Madras*	mədras 12
library	kwtwb-xana 16	*make*	kərna, bənana 6; (caus.) bənvana 1, 19
lie	pəṛna 12, 17; leṭna, 15, 17	*— uproar*	ʃor məcana 28
life	jan 12; zyndəgi 16	*male*	nər 1
		man	mərd, admi 1
lifelong	wmr bhər 27	*man-eating*	adəm xwr 12
light (weight)	həlka	*manage to*	pana 11
to —	jəlana 9	*mango*	am 3
lightning	byjli 8, 24	*manly*	mərdana 27
like	sa 22	*manner*	tərəh, təriqa 27
line	layn (mil.) 28	*mansion*	məkan 7, 20
listen	swnna 1, 18	*mare*	ghoṛi 3
little	thoṛa 28; kəm 13	*market*	bazar 7; məndi 24
a —	kwch 14; zəra 7		
liver	kəleja 21	*marriage*	ʃadi 18
load	ladna 6	*marry*	ʃadi kərna 18
loaded, be	lədna 19	*master*	malyk 11
loan	qərz 9	*(owner)*	
lock-up	hajət 16	*— (teacher)*	wstad 1
long	ləmba 2	*match*	diasəlai 23
loose	ḍhila 9	*to —*	jəvab meŋ hona 15
lose	khona 21		
— game	harna 10, 21	*matter*	bat, əmr 27
lost	khoya hua 11	*no —*	pərva, mwzayqa 24
be —	jata rəyhna 8		
lot	nəsib 7, 10	*maund*	mən 25, 26
love	mohəbbət 18	*means*	təriqa, zəria 27
to —	pyar kərna 10; cahna 13	*medicine*	dəva 11
		meet	mylna 21

meeting	mwlaqat 21, 28	*morning*	swbəh 9
— (*assembly*)	jəlsa 16	*mosque*	məsjyd 26
melon	xərbuza 24	*mother*	ma, maŋ 1
memorial	yadgar 20	*mountain*	pəhaɽ 9
memory	yad 13	*mouse*	cuhi 10
mention	zykr kərna 18	*mouth*	mwŋh 21
merciless	berəyhm 18	*move*	chwʈna 11
mercy	rəyhmət 1;	*movement*	hərkət 1
	rəyhm 18	*mule*	xəccər 18
messenger	cəprasi 18	*Muslim*	mwsəlman 18,
method	təriqa 27		26
middle	bicvala 26	*museum*	əjayb-xana 10
middle-aged	ədheɽ 27	*must*	pəɽna 12
midst	bic 26; dərmiyan	*mustard*	rai 24
	27	*mustard-pot*	raidani 25
mile	mil 7, 26	*mutually*	apəs meŋ 8
milk	dudh 2		
milkman	gəvala 6		
mind	ji 1, 11		
minute	mynəʈ 24	**N**	
mirror	ʃiʃa 22		
mischief	ʃərarət 28	*nail*	kil 11
misconduct	bədcəlni 17	*naked*	nənga 27
miser	kənjus 22	*narrate*	bəyan kərna 11
Miss	myssahb 20	*nation*	qəwm 24
miss	xali jana 28	*nature*	fytrət 25
mist	kohra 17	*naturally*	qwdrətən
mix	mylna 21; xəlt	*near*	pas, qərib, nəz-
	məlt hona 28;		dik 27
	mylana (tr.) 21	*nearest*	səb se nəzdik 26
moment	dəm 24; ləmha	*necessarily*	zərur 5
	27	*necessary*	zərur 11; zəruri
money	rwpia, rwpəya 21		24; cahie 11, 13
monkey	bəndər 10	*neck*	gəla 11
month	məhina 11	*needle*	sui 10
monthly	mahvari 27	*needless*	fwzul 12
moon	caŋd 22	*neighbourhood*	pəɽos 24
moonlight	caŋdni 22	*never*	kəbhi nəhiŋ 27
more	zyada, bəɽhkər 2	*new*	nəya 15
the —	juŋ juŋ 17	*news*	xəbər 25
— *or less*	kəm o beʃ 29	good —	xwʃxəbəri 24
		newspaper	əxbar 7

next	əgla, dusra, aynda 27	*office*	afys, dəftər 4, 21
night	rat 1	*officer*	əfsər 12
night long	rat bhər 27	*ogress*	bhwtni 22
noble	ʃərif 20	*oil*	tel 11
noise	ʃor 8; ɣwl ʃor 28	*old*	buɽha 3; bwḍḍha 27
nonsense (*to utter*)	bəkna, bəkvas kərna 10 ,12	*old-time*	pwrana 4
noon	do pəyhr 21	*only*	syrf 8
not	na, nəhiŋ 5	*open*	khwlna (intr.) 9, 19; kholna (tr.) 9, 19
note (*money*)	noṭ 18		
notwithstand-ing	bavwjud 8, 25	*opinion*	rae 14
		in — of	ke nəzdik 27
now	əb 5	*opium*	əfim 9
nowadays	aj kəl 27	*opportunity*	məwqa 16
nowhere	kəhiŋ nəhiŋ 27	*opposition*	mwqabələh 8; ke xylaf 27
number	tadad 26; nəmbər 11	*oppressor*	zalym 23
nurture	palna 20	*order*	hwkm 9
		— (send for)	məngvana 9
		orderly	baqayda 18
	O	*origin*	əsl 24
		ornament	zevər 10
O that	kaʃ 15	*other*	dusra 4
oar	cəppu 21	*otherwise*	nəhiŋ to 15
obedience	fərmaŋbərdari 18	*ought*	cahie 13
		outside	bahər 8
obey	bat manna 18	*overcome*	ɣalyb hona 14
object	ɣərəz 13	*oversight*	bhul 16
to —	etyraz kərna, 18	*owl*	wllu 10
oblige	məmnun kərna 18	*own*	əpna 3
		owner	malyk 11
obliged	məmnun 29		
obstinacy	zydd 17		
obtain	pana, hasyl kər-na, hath lana 11		**P**
obviously	zahyrən 29	*p.m.*	ʃam 26
occasion	dəfa 27	*page*	səfha 10
occupied	məsruf 9	*pagri*	pəgɽi 9
occur	vaqe hona 15	*pain*	dərd 15
o'clock	bəja 26	*to —*	dwkhna (intr.) 7

paint	rəng ləgana 11	permitted	jayz hona 26
pair	joɽa	perplexed	pərefan 17
in pairs	do do kərke 25	person	admi 1; ʃəxs 21
paisa	pəysa 25	perspiration	pəsina 29
palace	məyhəl 9	perverse	zyddi 17
palate	talu 11	phial	ʃiʃi 17
palm tree	taɽ 23	picture	təsvir 6
paper	kaɣəz 17, 28	piece	ʈwkɽa 21
—, piece of	pərca 17	pillar-box	ɖak-bəks 17
pardon, ask	mwafi maŋgna 17	pitcher	ghəɽa 15
		pity	rəyhm kərna 21
parents	ma bap 3; valy-dəyn 6	place	jəgəh 11, 27
		plague	taun 24, 28
park	məydan 9	plainly	saf 23
part	hyssa 26	plaintiff	mwddəi 20
partridge	titər 16	plane	həvai jəhaz, təiyara 21
pass (tr.)	bəsər kərna 16; gwzarna 28	plant	pəwda 11
patch	pəyvənd 11	play	khelna 6
patient, be	səbr kərna 15	poet	ʃayr 17
patriot	vətən-dost 20	pole	dəndi 21
patron	mwrəbbi 20	police	pwlys 16
pattern	nəmuna 22	polite	baədəb 29
paw	pənja 17	pony	ʈəʈʈu 9
pay	əda kərna 9, 18	poor	ɣərib 3; fəqir 13
pear	naʃpati 20	nurturer	ɣərib-pərvər 20
pearl	moti 1	of —	
pen	qələm 12	population	abadi 24
pencil	pynsyl 2	position	ohda 20
penknife	caqu 20	possessions	mylkiət 19
people	log 4	possibility	ymkan 14
— (nation)	qəwm 24	possible	mwmkyn 13
perfect	sahyb-e kəmal 20	post	ɖak meŋ ɖalna 14
perforce	məjburən 29; xa(h) məxa(h) 13, 29	postman	ɖakvala 11
		postpone	məwquf kərna 14
perhaps	ʃayəd 5	pound	adh ser 25
period	ərsa, əsr, mwddət 27	practice	məʃq kərna 12
		praise	tarif kərna 12, 18
permit	yjazət dena 11	praiseworthy	tarif ke qabyl 27

pray	nəmaz pəɽhna 18	*quickness*	jəldi 1
preparation	təiyari 9	*quiet*	cwp 8; cwpka 15
present	tohfa 11	*— (of animal)*	myskin 3
— (adj.)	hazyr 20;		
	məwjud 1, 20		
prevail	ɣalyb hona 14		R
previously	age, pəyhle,		
	peʃtər 27	*rabbit*	xərgoʃ 25
price	qimət, dam 25	*rain*	meŋh, baryʃ 11
priceless	be-bəha 18	*to —*	bərəsna (intr.) 11
prison	thana 16		bərsana (tr.)
prisoner	qəydi 18	*raise*	wʈhana 9
prize	ynam 11	*Raja*	raja 1
probably	ɣalybən 4	*Ramazan*	rəmzan 26
problem	məsla 20	*rank*	səf (mil.) 28
proceed	bəɽhna, cəlna 11	*rascal*	bədmaʃ 23
produced	pəyda hona 8	*reach*	pəwhŋcna 7
promise	vada kərna 11,	*read*	pəɽhna 7
	18	*ready*	təiyar 7, 12
promising	honhar 18	*ready-made*	bəna bənaya 28
proper	mwnasyb 7	*real*	həqiqi 16
property	mylkiət 19;	*reality*	əsl 24
	mal 29	*reason*	bays, səbəb,
propose	təjviz kərna 18,		vəjəh 27
	29	*reckoning*	ʃwmar 16
provisions	səwda 14	*recommenda-*	syfaryʃ 20
punctually	vəqt pər 14	*tion*	
punishment	səza 27	*recover one-*	səmbhəlna 16
pupil	ʃagyrd 9	*self*	
purpose	qəsd 28; ɣərəz 13	*refuse*	ynkar kərna 9
push	dhəkelna 17	*regard to*	lehaz 24
put	rəkhna 10;	*regiment*	pəlʈən 28
	ɖalna 11	*regular*	bazabta 18;
— out	nykalna 19		baqayda 29
		relate	bəyan kərna 6
		reliable	motəbər 27
	Q	*religion*	məzhəb 9
		remain	rəyhna 6, 8
quantity	qədr 23	*remaining*	baqi 26
quarrelsome	jhəgɽalu 17	*remember*	yad kərna 13
quick	jəld 2	*remind*	yad dylana 11

E

repair	mərəmmət kər-	*rude*	beədəb 29
	na 9, 18; (caus.)	*ruler*	raja 1
	19	*rumour*	əfva(h) 24
repent	pəchtana 27	*run*	dəwɽna 2
represent	ərz kərna 18	*rupee*	rwpia, rwpəya 1
reprove	mələmət kərna	*rural*	dehati 12
	18		
request	dərxast kərna 18		
resemble	mylna (jwlna)21	S	
resound	guŋjna 12		
respect of	bənysbət 27	*sack*	bori 6
responsibility	zymma 27	*sacrifice*	isar kərna 29
responsible	zymmedar 27	*sad*	wdas 16; mayus
rest	aram kərna 29		20
restless, be	becəyni kərna	*safe, be*	bəcna 16
	11	*safeguard*	hyfazət kərna 18
result	nətija 7	*sake of, for*	ke lie 29; ki
return	ləwɽna 7		xatyr 20, 24
revenue	malgwzari 18	*salary*	tənxa(h) 27
reward	ynam 11	*salt*	nəmək 25, 29
rice	cavəl 8	*salt-cellar*	nəməkdan 25
rich	əmir 13; dəwlət-	*sand*	ret
	mənd 21	*sandalwood*	səndəl 19
— (*of soil*)	zərxez 29	*save*	bəcana 16
rider	səvar 1	*saved, be*	bəcna 7
rifle	rəyfl 21	*saw*	ara 15
right	dayaŋ 9	*scarcely*	ʃayəd hi 7, 23
ripe	pəkka 3	*scarf*	gwlubənd 29
ripple	ləyhr 9	*scene*	mənzər 9
rise	wɽhna 7	*score*	koɽi 25
risk	xətra 16	*search*	ɖhuŋɖhna 21;
river	dərya 1; nəddi 7		tələʃ kərna 18
road	rəsta, rasta 17;	*seashore*	sahyl
	sərək 28; ra(h)21	*season*	məwsəm 12
rod	ɖənɖi 11	*seat*	kwrsi 22
roof	chət 1	*second*	dusra 4
room	kəmra 3	*see*	dekhna 6, 19
rose	gwl 23	*seed*	bij 13
rotten	səɽa 16	*seer*	ser 25, 26
row	cəppu marna 18;	*self*	ap, xwd 20
	khena 27	*selfish*	xwdɣərəz 25

sell	becna 12, 19	*short*	mwxtəsər 27
be sold	bykna 19	*in —*	yərəz
send	bhejna 12	*shout*	cyllana 15;
— for	məngvana 19		pwkarna 17
— word	kəyhla bhejna17	*show*	təmaʃa 10, 27
senseless	behoʃ 17	*to —*	dykhana 19
separate	jwda 24	*side*	tərəf 25, 27
sepoy	sypahi 21	*silken*	reʃmi 19
serious	əhəmm 5	*silver*	caɳdi 10
servant	nəwkər 1, 4, 28	*simplicity*	sadəgi 8
service	xydmət 18, 29	*sin*	gwna(h) 13
	nəwkəri 20	*since*	cuɳky 25
session	yjlas 16	*sincerity*	xwlus 18
set (sun)	ywrub hona 26	*with —*	səcce dyl se 18
— out	rəvana hona 12;	*sing*	gana 11, 27
	rwxsət hona 18	*singer*	gəvəiya 11
settle in	bəsna, swkunət	*sink*	ɖubna 15, 17
	kərna 12	*sir*	ap 5; jənab,
— with	səməjhna 21		hwzur, sahəb,
settled	qərar pana,		sahyb, miaɳ 20
	fəysla hona 11	*sister*	bəyhn 1, 15
several	kəi 3; cənd 14	*sit*	bəyʈhna 12, 17
severe	səxt 5	*situated*	vaqe hona 26
shady	saedar 9	*skill*	məharət 24
shaft	ɖənɖi 21	*sky*	asman 1
shake	hylana (tr.)	*slap*	təmaɳca marna
— hands	hath mylana 21		18
shame	ʃərm 9	*slapped*	təmaɳca khana
sharp	tez 7		16
sheen	cəmək 22	*sleep*	niɳd 8
sheep	bheɽ 21	*to —*	sona 6, 8
sheet	cadər 21	*put to —*	swlana 19
shelf	taq 4	*slowly*	ahysta 27
shell-fire	gola-bari 11	*small*	choʈa 2
ship	jəhaz 6	*smile*	mwskərana 7
shiver	kaɳpna 21	*smoke*	dhuaɳ 23
shoe	juti 6	*to —*	pina
shoot, go to	ʃykar khelna 27	*(tobacco)*	
shop	dwkan 11	*snake*	saɳp 5
— keeper	bənia 9; dwkan-	*snatch*	chinna 15, 17
	dar 25	*snow*	bərf 17

E*

street	kuca, bazar 4		**T**
strength	qwvvət 21; taqət 29; zor 11	*table*	mez 1
stretch	bəɽhana 17	— *servant*	xydmətgar 9
strike	marna 28	*tail*	dwm 1
stroke	var 28;	*take*	lena 9, 17
— (*swimming*)	hath marna 18	— *away*	lejana 9
strong	məzbut 4	— *out*	nykalna 16
— (*of tea*)	tez 2	*talent*	məlka 24
student	talyb-ə ylm 19	*talk*	bat kərna 2
stumble	ʈhokər khana 16	*tank*	təlao 26
subscription	cənda 17	*taxi*	ʈəyksi 9
success	kamyabi 7	*tea*	ca, cae 2, 10
successful	kamyab 4	*teach*	pəɽhana 1, 19
such	əysa 9, 23	*teacher*	wstad 6
— *and such*	fwlaŋ 21	*teapot*	caedan 10
suddenly	dəfətən 17; əcanək 9 yəkayək 11	*tear*	phəʈna (intr.) 9; phaɽna (tr.) 19
sugar	cini, ʃəkər 2	*temple*	məndər 27
suit	suʈ 15, 21	*than*	se 2
summer	gərmioŋ ka məwsəm 14	*thank*	ʃwkria kərna 18
summon	bwlana 9; bwla bhejna 17	*then*	təb, to 27
		there	vəhaŋ 3, 23
sun	surəj 7	*therefore*	ys lie 19
sunset	məɣryb 29	*thick*	moʈa 4
sunshine	dhup 15	*thief*	cor 11
support	səhara 15	*thin*	dwbla 4
suppressed, be	dəbna 24	*thing*	ciz 3
surely	zərur 21	*think*	yəwr kərna 6; socna 6, 7
surface	sətəh 26	*thirsty*	pyasa 10
surrender	əsleha ḍalna 17	*thorn*	xar 23; kaŋʈa
sustenance	pərəstyʃ 1	*thoughtfully*	yəwr se 6
swagger	əkəɽna 15	*thread*	dhaga 13
sweet	miʈha 2	*threefold*	tygwna 25
swimmer	təyrne vala 18	*thrifty*	kəm xərc, ky- fayət ʃyar 29
sword	təlvar 16	*throne*	təxt 17
sycophancy	zəmanasazi 29	*thunder*	gərəj 12
sympathise	həmdərdi kərna 16, 18	*to* —	gərəjna 8
		thus	yuŋ 23

tiger	ʃer 1	*tube*	nəli 25
time	vəqt 11; zəmana 8, 27	*turn*	ghumna (intr.); ghwmana (tr.) 9
— and again	bar bar 28	*twofold*	dwgna, duna 25
tiny	nənha 22	*typhoon*	twfan 24
tire	thək jana 14, 28		
tobacco	təmbaku 23		
to-day	aj 27		

U

toe	paoŋ ki wngli 23		
together	ek sath 10; apəs meŋ 8; mylkər 21	*ugly*	bədsurət 29
		uncle	cəca 1
		understand	səməjhna 10
to-morrow	kəl 2	*understanding*	səməjh 10
tongue	zəban 11	*unfortunate*	bədnəsib 29;
too	bhi 5		kəmbəxt 22, 29
tooth	daṇt 7	*unjust*	naynsaf 29
— paste	mənjən 25	*unlucky*	bədbəxt 29;
torn	phəṭa 9		bədqysmət 22
be —	phəṭ jana 9, 19	*unnoticed*	aŋkh bəcakər 16
tour	səyr 18	*unread*	ənpəṛh 16
towards	ki tərəf 9	*unripe*	kəcca 3
trace	pəta 11	*until*	jəb tək 27
trade	len den 9, 28	*untruth*	jhuṭi bat 13;
train	rel 6		jhuṭ 12
transient	cəndroza 24	*urgent*	zəruri 24
traveller	mwsafyr 11	*use*	kam meŋ lana 9;
traverse	təy kərna 20		kam lena 20;
tread	paoŋ 27		ystemal kərna 18
treasurer	xəzanci 20		
treat	peʃ ana 16	*useful*	kam ka 2; kam ana 9
tree	dərəxt 7		
tremble	kaŋpna 21, 28	*usurp*	yəsəb kərna 17
tress	gesu 22	*utterly*	bylkwl 28
trice	an 28		
trouble, give	təklif dena		
—, take	təklif kərna 7, 20	V	
trousers	pətlun 11		
true	səc 23; səcca 27	*vegetable*	tərkari 19
trust, in	həvale 27	*velvet*	məxməl 23
to —	yəqin kərna 18	*verdant*	həra 28
try	koʃyʃ kərna 15	*very*	bəwht 2

village	gaoŋ 5; qəsba 17	*way*	rəsta, rasta 4
virulence	zor ʃor se 28	*way* (*manner*)	təwr 11; tərəh
visible	dykhai dena 11		27
voice	avaz 10; zəban	*weak*	kəmzor 4
	24	*weakness*	kəmzori 15
		wealthy	dəwlətmənd 19
		weapons	əsleha 17
	W	*wear*	pəyhnna 27
		weave	bwnna 10
wages	wjrət, tələb 17	*week*	həfta 27, 29
wait	yntyzar kərna	*weekly*	həftevar 27
	19	*weep*	rona
waiter	xydmətgar 9	*make* —	rwlana 19
wake	jagna 19; jəgana	*weigh*	tolna (tr.)
	(tr.) 19	*weight*	vəzən
walk	səyr kərna 11,	*well*	əcchi tərəh 19;
	18		xub 7 ; xəyr 12
wall	dival, divar 2	*west*	məɣryb 29
wander	mare mare	*what*	kya, kəwn 3
	phyrna 18	*when*	jəb 27; kəb
want	maŋgna 8		(interr.) 23
war	ləɽai 27	*whenever*	jəbhi, jəb kəbhi
wardrobe	əlmari 4		27
warship	jəngi jəhaz	*where*	jəhaŋ 8; kəhaŋ
wash	dhona 19		(interr.) 4, 23
— (*caus.*)	dhwlana 19	*wherever*	jəhaŋ kəhiŋ 8
washed, be	dhwlna 19	*whether . . . or*	cahe . . . cahe,
washerman	dhobi 6		kya . . . kya,
—'*s quarter*	dhobi paɽa 19		xa(h) . . . xa(h)
washing-place	dhobi ghaʈ 19		13
wasp	bhyʈ 18	*which*	jo 3; kəwn
waste	rəddi 9		(interr.) 3
watch	ghəɽi 19	*whilst*	jəb tək 27
watchmaker	ghəɽi saz 19	*whirl*	cəkkər 17 ;
watchman	cəwkidar 16	*to* —	cəkrana 11
water, to	pani dena 11	*whisper*	dəbi zəban se
water carrier	behyʃti, pani-		kəyhna 24
	vala 12	*whistle*	siʈi 19
waterproof	bərsati 25	*white*	səfed 9
wave	ləyhrana (intr.)	*whither*	jydhər, kydhər
	15		(interr.) 23

who	jo 3; kəwn (interr.) 3
whoever	jo koi 4
whole	təmam 7; sara 6
why	kyoŋ 27
wicked	ʃərir 18
wide	cəwɽa 2
wife	bibi 13; begəm 17
willy-nilly	xa(h) məxa(h) 13
win	jitna 10
wind	həva 7
window	khyɽki 7
wipe	poŋchna 29
wire	tar 9
wise	dana 1; əqlmənd 22
wish	xahyʃ 27
to —	cahna 7, 13
without	be, byn, bəɣəyr 29
witness	gəva(h) 27
woman	əwrət 1
wonderful	əjib 10
wood	ləkɽi 2
woodman	ləkəɽhara 21
word	ləfz 28; hərf 25
work	kam 1
workman	məzdur 11
— (journey-man)	mystri 15.

world	dwnya 6
worship	puja kərna, ybadət kərna 18
worth	qədr 23
worthy	qabyl 12, 18, 27
would that	kaʃ 15
wound	coʈ 11
wounded	zəxmi 10
wretched	kəmbəxt 22
wrinkle	bəl 17
wrist-watch	hath ghəɽi 21
write	lykhna 8
writing	lykha 15
wrong	ɣələt

Y

yawn	əngɽai 7
year	sal 7; bərəs 24
yellow	zərd, pila 11
yes	haŋ 2
yesterday	kəl 2
yet	təw bhi, phyr bhi 7
Yogi	yogi 12
yoked	jwtna 11
young	jəvan 4; nəw-jəvan 27

Z

| zoo | cyɽiaxana 20 |

KEY TO EXERCISES

ENGLISH—HINDUSTANI

Exercise I

1. lərke ka hath. 2. admi ka kan. 3. lərki ke bal. 4. lərke ki zəban. 5. səvar ke ghoɽe ka swm. 6. lərkioŋ ki maŋ. 7. ghoɽe ki dwm ka ek bal. 8. əwrətoŋ ka kam. 9. admi ki hərkəteŋ. 10. lərkoŋ ke hathoŋ meŋ. 11. ʃeroŋ ke səroŋ pər. 12. ghəroŋ ke dərvazoŋ tək.

Exercise II

1. yeh tez ghoɽa həy, kəl twmhare ghoɽe se tez dəwɽa. 2. yeh pynsyl choʈi həy lekyn voh əwr bhi choʈi həy. 3. yeh pani taza həy—ji nəhiŋ, taza nəhiŋ (həy). 4. yeh bəɽi mez həy, bəwht bəɽi həy, ghər meŋ səb se bəɽi həy. 5. meri ca tez həy, bəwht tez həy. 6. mere qəyhve meŋ zyada ʃəkər həy, bəwht miʈha həy. 7. twmhari mez ləmbi əwr cəwɽi həy, meri mez se ləmbi həy, bəwht kam ki həy.

Exercise III

1. yəh əccha admi həy. 2. voh kya bwra lərka tha. 3. voh ghoɽi myskin həy, voh mere ghoɽe se kali həy. 4. twmhare hath meŋ kya həy—meri choʈi beʈi ki gwɽia həy. 5. yeh kəwn admi həy—yeh ek ɣərib əwrət həy. 6. dərvaze pər kəwn log the—voh əndhe admi the. 7. ws ke hath meŋ kya həy—ek choʈi kytab həy. 8. kəl voh səb vəhaŋ the. 9. yeh meri əpni kytab həy, ws ki nəhiŋ. 10. voh ws ki əpni kytab həy.

Exercise IV

1. voh kəwn admi həy—voh mera dost həy. 2. dusra admi kəwn həy—voh mera pwrana nəwkər həy. 3. jo koi bhi mehnati ho voh ɣalybən kamyab hoga. 4. voh xubsurət lərki hogi. 5. yeh twmhari ʈopi həy—nəhiŋ meri ʈopi kali həy. 6. yeh kys ka ghər həy—mere dost ka həy, voh kuce (bazar) meŋ səb se uŋca həy.

Exercise V

1. yeh kytna bəɽa ghoɽa həy ; ghoɽa bəɽa janvər hota həy.
2. voh yəhaŋ thi lekyn əb yəhaŋ nəhiŋ. 3. yeh mwʃkyl bat
həy lekyn koi mayus na ho. 4. xəbərdar—ʃayəd vəhaŋ saŋp ho.
5. ys mwlk meŋ səxt sərdi hoti (pəɽti) həy—kəbhi kəbhi bəwht
gərmi bhi hoti həy. 6. koi ys kəmre meŋ zərur tha—koi ys
kəmre meŋ zərur aya hoga. 7. ys kəmre meŋ kysi ko nə ane
do—koi ws əndhere kəmre meŋ nəhiŋ jaega. 8. voh dehati aj
yəhaŋ kyoŋ ae həyŋ. 9. yəqin kəro ya nə kəro yeh səc həy.
10. ʃayəd ləɽka yəhaŋ ho əwr ws ki maŋ bhi. 11. kya hua
(kya bat həy)—ghər meŋ koi nəhiŋ həy. 12. ws ke valydəyn
(maŋ bap) xwʃ həyŋ—voh xwʃ rəheŋ.

Exercise VI

1. gəvale ki gaeŋ kəhaŋ cərti həyŋ. 2. ws ki gaeŋ əb vəhaŋ
cər rəhi həyŋ. 3. qwli kys qysm ke kam kərte həyŋ. 4. qwli
səxt kam kərte həyŋ. 5. qwli bəɽa səxt kam kər rəhe the.
6. yeh dhobi əccha kam kərta həy ; kəpɽe saf kərta həy, voh əb
kəpɽe saf kər rəha həy. 7. həm dyn ko kam kərte həyŋ, əwr
rat ko sote həyŋ. 8. wstad bol rəha həy—jəb wstad bolta
həy to ləɽke swnte həyŋ. 9. jəb wstad bol rəhe the to ləɽke
bateŋ kər rəhe the. 10. mahigir qyssa (kəhani) kəyh (bəta)
rəha tha. 11. voh bazar ja rəha tha, ws ki bəyhn ws ke sath
na thi. 12. qwli boriaŋ rel se leja rəhe həyŋ, wn ko jəhaz pər
ladeŋge. 13. ləɽko twm kəl kya kər rəhe the. 14. bavərci
khana pəka rəha həy.

Exercise VII

1. mwnasyb həy ky twm jao. 2. məyŋ jauŋ—nəhiŋ, yəhaŋ
rəho. 3. voh cəla gəya, ʃayəd phyr ae (aega). 4. ymtehan ka
nətija təiyar həy ; ʃayəd twm voh kəl ke əxbar meŋ pəɽhoge.
5. bəytho ; yəhaŋ bəyþhie ; ap ys kwrsi pər bəyþhie. 6. xəbərdar ;
ʃayəd voh janvər twmhəŋ kaʈe ; ws ke daŋt bəwht tez həyŋ.
7. voh kwrsi se wʈhkər khyɽki ke pas gəya. 8. voh ytna bəɽa bhi
hokər ḍər ke mare bhaga. 9. əgərcy surəj nykla hwa tha phyr
bhi həva þhənḍi thi. 10. ws ka məkan kuce meŋ səb se bəɽa həy ;
bazar se do mil ke fasle pər həy. 11. kwtte goʃt khate həyŋ ;
bylliaŋ dudh piti həyŋ. 12. bylli dudh pikər bahər jaegi, lekyn
kwtta goʃt khakər bhitər rəhega. 13. ek həfta hua ky voh
yəhaŋ pəwhŋca. 14. kya yeh nəddi sal bhər bəyhti rəyhti həy.

EXERCISE VIII

1. voh khəṛi həy ; voh khəṛi rəhi ; voh yəhaŋ rəhegi. 2. voh cavəl khata həy ; voh kha nəhiŋ rəha həy ; voh khata rəyhta həy ; voh khata rəha. 3. padri sahəb gyrje ja rəhe həyŋ ; voh gyrje jate həyŋ ; voh gyrje a rəhe həyŋ. 4. voh gəyhra gəṛha khod rəha həy ; məzdur ek gəyhra gəṛha khod rəhe the ; voh gəyhre gəṛhe ydhər wdhər khod rəhe the. 5. twm kya kər rəhe ho ; twm kəl kya kər rəhe the ; twm kəl kya kər rəhe hoge. 6. voh əcchi (xub) dəwṛti həy ; voh dəwṛti rəyhti həy ; voh dəwṛti rəhi. 7. ek admi ja rəha tha ; ws ke sath ek choṭa kwtta tha. 8. vərzyʃ se bədən təndrwst rəyhta həy. 9. bəhadwr kysi se nəhiŋ dərta. 10. fəwj ydhər a rəhi həy ; ws meŋ rysala bhi həy əwr pyada pəltən bhi. 11. voh təmam rat pəyhre pər rəha. 12. voh bəcca ro rəha həy ; voh kyoŋ ro rəha həy ; voh həmeʃa rota həy ; voh rat dyn rota həy ; voh hoŋt nykalkər rota həy. 13. voh dəftər roz jata həy ; voh dəftər se ʃam ko ata həy ; voh əb a rəha həy ; voh ata rəyhta həy.

EXERCISE IX

1. yəhaŋ ao ; idhər ao ; jəld (jəldi) ao ; ahysta (ahysta) ao. 2. vəhaŋ kəwn ja rəha həy ; mehrbani kərke jaie ; wdhər jao ; piche piche jao (həṭo). 3. yeh kytab lo ; twm yeh kytab loge ? məyŋ ys ko nəhiŋ luŋga. 4. mwjhe mwaf kijie, məyŋ əpna kam kəruŋga. 5. mere lie (vaste) kali ṭopi lao ; ws ki səfed pəgṛi lao. 6. bolo, bolo ; məyŋ kya boluŋ ; ws se yeh kəho. 7. ys kəmre meŋ əndhera həy ; mom-bətti jəlao, bəlky bətti jəlao ; voh bətti bwjhao. 8. sidhe jao (bəṛho) ; daeŋ hath jao (ghumo) ; baeŋ ghumo (jao) ; ghumo ; gəṛi ghwmao. 9. dərvaza kholo ; khyṛki bənd kəro. 10. bəyra, bavərci ko (se) kəho (bolo) ky yəhaŋ ae ; hwzur, bavərci ghər meŋ nəhiŋ (həy) ; voh bazar gəya həy lekyn jəldi (thoṛi der bad) ləwṭega (vapəs aega). 11. jənab, aj məchli ke tin qysm ke khane həyŋ ; əccha, mwjhe wbli hwi məchli pəsənd həy, lekyn ws ke lie əbhi kəho ta ky der na ho jae. 12. ek nəwkər bwlao ; gəṛi bwlaie (bwlvaie) ; gəṛi məngao (məngvao). 13. voh roz kwch lykha kərta həy. 14. məyŋ hər roz fəjr ko jagta huŋ əwr səvere hi uṭhta huŋ. 15. voh hər roz do pəyhr ko ṭyfyn khaya kərta həy. 16. məyŋ roz swbh tin ghənṭe pəṛha kərta huŋ.

Exercise X

1. mwjhe ek kytab do ; kytab (ko) dijie ; mehrbani kərke yeh kytab əpne beţe ko dijie. 2. maŋ ko beţi se pyar həy əwr beţi ko əpni maŋ se. 3. cil choţe janvəroŋ ka ʃykar kərti həy ; wllu cuhioŋ ka ʃykar kər rəha həy ; bylli cuhi ko khaegi. 4. ek nəwkər bwlao; bəyra ko bwlao ; məyŋ əpne nəwkər ko bwlauŋga. 5. bəyra ko kəho ky qələm dəvat mez pər rəkhe ; kysi ne ys dəvat ko mez pər rəkha hoga. 6. syrf thoɽi si roţi ghər meŋ thi ; memsahb ne kwch əwr məngai. 7. əwrəteŋ bhukhi pyasi thiŋ ; wnhoŋ ne roţi khai əwr dudh pia ; wnhoŋ ne bəwht sa ţhənda pani pia. 8. ws ne səb nəwkəroŋ ko ghər meŋ bwlaya. 9. ws ne ek dyn ki chwţţi maŋgi. 10. məyŋ ne ys kytab ke cənd səfhe pəɽhe həyŋ. 11. twm ne əpne dost ko kəl cyţţhi lykhi ? 12. twm ne əjayb-xane meŋ kya kya əjib cizeŋ dekhiŋ.

Exercise XI

1. ws ne bəyţhkər ek qyssa karxane ke bare meŋ bəyan kərna ʃwru kia. 2. ek admi bat kərne ləga, dusra pəɽhne ləga. 3. voh apəs meŋ bateŋ kərne ləge. 4. twm ko yeh bat əcchi ləgti həy ya (ky) nəhiŋ. 5. dekho to ky tala dərvaze pər həy. 6. ys kam meŋ syrf thoɽi der ləgegi. 7. həm baɽ ki səyr kərne ləge ; thoɽi der bad meŋh bərəsne ləga. 8. ws ko zwkam həy, voh bəwht khaŋsta həy. 9. yəhaŋ ane meŋ tin ghəŋţe se zyada nəhiŋ ləgeŋge. 10. ws ne həmeŋ əpne xubsurət baɽ meŋ hər roz səyr kərne ki yjazət di. 11. voh əpne bəccoŋ ko əysi kytabeŋ pəɽhne nəhiŋ deta. 12. malyk ne wse tin məhine ki chwţţi di. 13. phaţək khwla həy ; bhitər jane ki yjazət nəhiŋ cahie. 14. məyŋ kam xətm kərne nəhiŋ paya. 15. voh ws pər hath tək ləgane nəhiŋ pae. 16. age ek bəɽa dərəxt tha, ws pər bəwht am ləge the ; wn meŋ se kwch pəkke the, əwr kwch zərd rəng pəkəɽne ləge the. 17. məyŋ ne hər jəgəh (caroŋ tərəf) dekha, lekyn koi dykhai na dia.

Exercise XII

1. twm ko ghər jana həy. 2. voh ghər jane-vali həy. 3. mwjh ko ek əccha ghoɽa xəridna həy. 4. əysi bevəqufi na kərna. 5. məyŋ yəhaŋ se nəhiŋ jane ka. 6. wse yeh saman lejane mat do—bəwht əccha, sahəb, məyŋ ws ko yjazət nəhiŋ

duŋga. 7. ytna xərc kərna fwzul həy. 8. ys kytab ke tin
səfhe roz pəṛhne se bəwht fayda hoga. 9. ws nəyhr ka gənda
pani pina əccha nəhiŋ həy. 10. ap chwṭṭi pər kəb jane-vale
həyŋ. 11. səfər kərna talim hasyl kərna həy. 12. voh sərdioŋ
ke bad ys mwlk meŋ rəyhne ki nəhiŋ. 13. voh rəvana hone
ko thi lekyn nəhiŋ gəi. 14. ws jəngəl meŋ ek adəm-xwr ʃer
həy, əfsər-e jəngəlat swbh səvere ws ka ʃykar kərne jaega.
15. dusre ki xatyr ya əpne mwlk ki xatyr jan deni tarif ke
qabyl həy. 16. məyŋ əysi fwzul bateŋ swnne ka nəhiŋ.

<h2>EXERCISE XIII</h2>

1. voh pəṛh rəha həy ; voh hər roz pəṛhta həy ; pəṛhne meŋ
ws ka dyl ləgta həy; voh pəṛha kərta həy; voh hər məhine
kəm se kəm ek mwʃkyl kytab pəṛhta həy ; pəṛhna ws ke nəzdik
xwʃi ki bat həy; ws ko əpne ymtehan ke lie bəwht pəṛhna həy ;
ʃagyrd hər dyn ek nəya səbəq pəṛha kərta həy ; voh kəl ka
səbəq pəṛh rəha həy ; yad kərne ke lie dyl ləgakər pəṛhna cahie ;
voh məjbur hokər pəṛhta həy. 2. ys wmed se bhi gwna(h) nə
kərna cahie ky nətija əccha hoga. 3. twm ko ys kytab ke tin
səfhe roz pəṛhne cahie(ŋ). 4. twm ko əpne ghoṛe ke sər pər nə
marna cahie. 5. ws ko nəyhr ka gənda pani na pina cahie.
6. ap chwṭṭi pər kəb jana cahte həyŋ. 7. məyŋ ys mwlk ki
zəban sikhni cahta huŋ ; jo jys mwlk meŋ rəhe wse ws mwlk ki
zəban sikhni cahie. 8. voh cahe na cahe ws ko yeh qərz ada
kərna pəṛega (zərur həy). 9. pəyhle twm ko koʃyʃ kərni cahie,
ws ke bad mwmkyn həy ky kamyabi ho. 10. hər ʃəxs ko
dusroŋ ki mədəd kərni mwnasyb həy.

<h2>EXERCISE XIV</h2>

1. kya voh aj vəhaŋ jà səkegi—kəl voh bazar ja nəhiŋ səki.
2. voh cəlne ki koʃyʃ kərta rəha lekyn cəl nə səka. 3. yeh ghoṛa
tez dəwṛ səkta həy, məgər voh zyada tez cəlta həy. 4. twm moṭər
cəla səkte ho—əgər nəhiŋ to sikho ; jəb twm sikh cwkoge to
cəlane meŋ xwʃi məyhsus kəroge. 5. twm ek dyn meŋ kəhaŋ
tək pəwhŋc səkte ho. 6. voh thək gəya ys lie age na bəṛh
səka. 7. jo kwch twm aj kər səkte ho kəl pər məwquf na kəro.
8. jəb məyŋ vəhaŋ pəwhŋca voh pəṛhna xətm kər cwke the.
9. saman xətm həy. 10. gərmi ka məwsəm xətm hua, cənd
dynoŋ bad voh ləwṭeŋge.

Exercise XV

1. voh həŋsti həŋsti axyrkar cəli gəi. 2. voh peṭi baŋdhte hue əwr hath meŋ kwlhaṛi lie dəwṛa aya. 3. ws ki aŋkheŋ təmaʃa dekhte dekhte thək gəiŋ. 4. ws admi ne koʃyʃ kərte kərte jan de di. 5. voh ṭopi hath meŋ lie pəwhŋci; bad meŋ dhup meŋ bəyṭhe hue voh xwʃ əwr lapərva hogəi. 6. ws ne cyllate hue ghəṛa bhəra. 7. voh dəstane pəyhne hue bahər gəi. 8. əgər voh jəldi aega to məyŋ bahər jauŋga; əgər voh jəldi ae to məyŋ bahər jauŋga; əgər voh jəldi na ata to məyŋ bahər na jata; kaʃ ky voh jəldi ae; voh ae nə ae məyŋ cəla jauŋga. 9. əgər voh jəldi aya hota to yeh kəbhi na hota; yeh kəyse ho səka. 10. həva ae twfan ae məyŋ ws pəhaṛ pər cəṛhuŋga. 11. nəwkər əpne malyk ke sath (ke həmra(h)) aya. 12. kaʃ ky mere ma bap yəhaŋ hote—voh yəhaŋ hote to mwjh se zyada koi xwʃ na hota.

Exercise XVI

1. admi xətre se bəcaya gəya. voh xətre se bəc gəya. 2. voh pəṛh lykh nəhiŋ səkta, ys lie ws ka ʃwmar ənpəṛhoŋ meŋ hoga. 3. voh kysi ciz se ṭhokər khakər gyr pəṛa əwr ws ka bazu ṭuṭ gəya. 4. ʃykari ne do titər ek kartus se mare (mar ḍale). 5. ys ləṛke ko kya kəyhte (kəyse pwkarte) həyŋ; voh əpne nam se nəhiŋ pwkara jata; yeh ləṛka swləyman ka həqiqi bhai nəhiŋ həy, swləyman ke bap ne ws ko mwtəbənna bənaya. 6. səmbhəlo (əpne ap ko səmbhalo), wdas na ho. 7. mwnasyb həy ky voh məʃhur səmjha jae əwr ws ki yzzət ho. 8. məyŋ ne bhul se yeh kia; mera qwsur mwaf kijie; nəhiŋ yeh twmhari lapərvai ka nətija tha; twm syrf wzr kər rəhe ho. 9. yeh kam mere lie bəwht mwʃkyl həy; mwjh se nəhiŋ kia jata.

Exercise XVII

1. yeh le lo; wn ke lie yeh lejao. 2. ws ciz ko mujhe do (de do); voh mujh ko de do; dwʃmən ne əpne əslyha (həthyar) ḍal die. 3. bəyṭho; bəyṭhie; məyŋ kəhaŋ bəyṭhuŋ; voh dərəxt ke nice (təle) bəyṭha həy. 4. yn səb cizoŋ ko əlmari ke taq pər rəkh do. 5. ḍakuoŋ ne ws ka (ki) sathi mar ḍala (ḍali). 6. kya, ws ne cyṭṭhiaŋ lykh diŋ jəyse məyŋ ne ws ko kəha tha. 7. ys ghəṛe ka pani pheŋk do. 8. voh səb bol wṭhe

ky həm təb tək na bəyɬheŋge jəb tək ky twm əpni bədcəlni ki
mwafi na maŋg lo. 9. kwtta sara məkkhən kha gəya. 10. voh
wmda dərəxt kys ne kaʈ ɖala həy. 11. həmla kərne-valoŋ ne kya
pwkara maro ya mar ɖalo. 12. bəndər kaɣəz (pərca) lie bhag
gəya lekyn məyŋ ne voh ws ke pənje se chin lia. 13. əpni
kytab le lijie ; məyŋ wse ap ko vapəs de rəha huŋ ; wse lene
ke lie hath jytni dur ho səke bəɽhaie ; kya, ap ne ws ko paya.

EXERCISE XVIII

1. ws ne ɣəyr-mwlki (əjnəbi) se əccha swluk (bərtao) kia.
2. mwjh pər ynayət kərke yse ɖak meŋ ɖal dijie. 3. məyŋ
ne xwlus se ws ka ʃwkria əda kia. 4. ws ne mwjhe pura vaqia
swnaya. 5. ws ne yeh kərke mwjhe məmnun kia. 6. ws ne
sərdar ki xydmət meŋ syr jhwkaya. 7. ws ne ws se vada kia
lekyn bad meŋ toɽ dia. 8. jəj sahb ne ws pər (wse) həzar rwpəya
jwrmana kia. 9. həm apəs meŋ ws ke bare meŋ gwftəgu kər
rəhe the. 10. jo kwch məyŋ ne yad kərne ko kəha kya twm
ko yad həy. kya twm ko yeh yad həy. 11. ws ka ymtehan
kəwn lega—yeh əbhi nəhiŋ malum, lekyn voh əgle (aynda ;
dusre) məhine meŋ ymtehan dega ; voh hyndostani meŋ qabyl
həy əwr kamyab zərur hojaega. 12. məyŋ ys bəyan ka yəqin
nəhiŋ kərta. 13. ws ko yaqin dyla do ky məyŋ ws ki mədəd
kəruŋga. 14. ʃadi ki təqrib meŋ (pər) dwlhən ne vada kia ky
dwlha se mohəbbət, yzzət əwr fərmaŋbərdari se peʃ aegi.
15. qəydi ne rəyhm ki dərxast ki.

EXERCISE XIX

1. ys talyb-e ylm ne yn kytaboŋ ko skul meŋ pəɽha ; voh yn
ko pəɽh cwka həy ; ws ka ymtehan ho cwka həy ys lie wn ko
bykvane ki koʃyʃ kərega. 2. məyŋ əpne beʈe ko hyndostani
pəɽhvata huŋ ; voh dyl ləgake ys zəban ko pəɽh rəha həy. 3. ws
ne dərəxt ko ek ləkɽhare se kəʈvaya jys ne ara əwr kwlhaɽi
ystemal ki (se kam lia) ; təb ws ne ws ko ek gaɽi pər lədvaya jys
ko ek məzbut ghoɽe ne khiŋca. 4. əwrət ne kəpɽe dhobi se ws
ke ghaʈ pər dhwlvae jo dhobipaɽe ke pas həy. 5. twm ne
mujh se ɬhik pəndra mynəʈ ka yntyzar kəraya. 6. garɖ ne
siʈi bəjai əwr rel chwʈjane ləgi. 7. dhobi se zyada təvəjjoh
ke sath ye reʃmi moza dhwlvao. 8. yuswf ko fəwran yəhan ane
ko kəyhla bhejo. 9. ws ke berəyhm pəkəɽne vale ne ws ko təmam

mylkiət se məyhrum kəraya. 10. ws ke kwtte ne mere þəɣice meŋ bəwht nwqsan pəwhŋcaya ; ws ki təvəjjoh ys tərəf fəwran kərao əwr ws se kəho ky sahyb ko ws pər bəwht ɣwssa həy. 11. aj rat ko məydan meŋ atyʃbazi hogi.

EXERCISE XX

1. twm ws ke beţe ho ; ws ke beţe beţiaŋ səb yəhaŋ məwjud həyŋ. 2. ghoɽe əwr gaeŋ dono ek hi khet meŋ cərte həyŋ. 3. əy beţe beţi meri bat swno. 4. am əwr naʃpatiaŋ dono mwjhe bəwht pəsənd həyŋ. 5. ws ke hath əwr wngliaŋ xubsurət həyn. 6. hyndostan meŋ gaeŋ nəhiŋ bəlky bəyl chəkɽe kheŋcte həyŋ. 7. məyŋ xwd aj vəhaŋ jane-vala huŋ (jauŋga). 8. əgər voh xwd rwpia nəhiŋ de səkta to ʃayəd ws ka bhai ws ke lie peʃgi dede. 9. log əpne əpne ghəroŋ ko ləwţe. 10. jənab, ap mere mwrəbbi həyŋ ; ynayət kərke ws ohde (nəwkəri) ke lie meri syfaryʃ kər dijie. 11. jənab, mehrbani kərke yeh məsla təy (həl) kərne meŋ mədəd dijie. 12. hər vətəndost əpne vətən ko səb mwlkoŋ se zyada pəsənd kərta həy. 13. mera dost syhhət ki xatyr əpne gaoŋ ko gəya həy. 14. mwddəi xwʃ hokər ədalət se gəya lekyn mwdda ələy mayus hokər rəyh gəya. 15. jənab, ap ke dərvaze (pər) ek ɣərib admi həy. 16. ws ke cal cələn ka xəyal rəkhte hue məyŋ ws ko qərz nəhiŋ dena cahta. 17. jənab, swbəh ka khana, jyse əngrez naʃta (hazyri) kəyhte həyŋ, təiyar həy. 18. ɣərib-pərvər, ap mere ma bap həyŋ ; ys bədqysməti ki halət meŋ meri mədəd kijie.

EXERCISE XXI

1. kya, ap ka əpna pəɽhne ka kəmra həy. 2. ap ke pas hath-ghəɽi həy—kya, yeh ţhik cəlti həy ya tez. 3. twmhəŋ jitkər kya ynam myla. 4. ws ne bygəɽkər cəppu toɽ dia. 5. ghoɽe bhage əwr dənɖi toɽ ɖali. 6. kəl voh mwjh ko cəwrahe pər myla. 7. jəb mwjhe fwrsət hogi to məyŋ ap se myluŋga (ap ki xydmət meŋ hazyr huŋga). 8. ws ke valydəyn nəhiŋ həyŋ. 9. jyn logoŋ ke dyl meŋ rəzaməndi (qənaət) ho wn ke lie voh ɣənimət həy. 10. ws ke pas kafi həy, lekyn bəwht zyada nəhiŋ. 11. do dyn hue ky meri hathghəɽi relgaɽi meŋ kho gəi. 12. mehrbani kərke mwjhe əpne dost se mylaie—ap ki mwlaqat se mwjhe bəwht xwʃi həy.

Exercise XXII

1. voh məzbut həy—voh rwstəm sa məzbut əwr bəhadwr həy
—ytna məzbut admi meri nəzər se kəbhi nəhiŋ gwzra—ws
jəysa məzbut koi nəhiŋ həy. 2. koi sa admi ane do. 3. pitəl
ki cəmək surəj ki rəwʃni ki tərəh thi (pitəl ki cəmək ki surəj ki si
rəwʃni thi). 4. əgərcy (go) voh qarun jəysa dəwlətmənd tha
lekyn (phyr bhi) voh kəmbəxt bədqysmət tha. 5. əgər məwqa
myla (mylega) to məyŋ qəbul kər luŋga. 6. ws ki səxavət
hatym ki si məʃhur thi. 7. ws ki surət təsvir ki si səjili (xubsurət)
thi (voh təsvir ka sa xubsurət tha). 8. ws ki surət caŋdni rat
ke caŋd ki si thi. 9. məyŋ kys kwrsi pər bəyʈhuŋ—jys pər
dyl (ji) cahe bəyʈhie. 10. ʃiʃe ke samne khəɽi hokər voh əpne
saŋp se kale gesu kənghi kər rəhi thi.

Exercise XXIII

1. jo chwri kaŋʈe draz meŋ hoŋ lao. 2. jo kwch məyŋ ne
twm ko (se) kəha voh kyoŋ nəhiŋ kia. 3. jəysa malyk vəysa
hi nəwkər. 4. jəysi voh xubsurət həy vəysi hi mehrban. 5. voh
ytna dwbla həy ky ws ki wngliaŋ diasəlai si həyŋ. 6. jys bavərci
ki syfaryʃ ap ne mwjh se ki thi voh bəɽa bədmaʃ həy. 7. jys
taɽ ke nice ap ys vəqt khəɽe həyŋ ws ki jəɽ meŋ saŋp ka byl həy.
8. jəhaŋ dhuaŋ hoga vəhaŋ ag zərur hogi. 9. ys botəl meŋ
wtni ʃərab nəhiŋ jytni kəl thi. 10. əfsər ne ws sypahi ko ynam
dia jys ne ws ki jan bəcai. 11. bylli ka pənja məxməl ki tərəh
mwlaym hota həy.

Exercise XXIV

1. hər koi ys ki koʃyʃ kər səkta həy lekyn hər ek məharət
təjryba ya məlka nəhiŋ rəkhta. 2. hər ek hyssa le. 3. ek ne
dusre se kəha həm apəs meŋ məʃvəra kəreŋ. 4. ys qysm ki
əfva(h) ka yəqin na kəro (kərna). 5. jyn logoŋ ko xwda ne ʃadi
meŋ mylaya həy wnheŋ koi ʃəxs jwda na kəre. 6. yeh həmari
qəwm ka moamla həy; əsl meŋ yeh təmam dwnya ke lie əhəmm
həy. 7. jəyse ek bheɽ kərti həy vəyse hi səb bheɽeŋ kərti həyŋ.
8. koi yeh pəsənd kərta həy, koi voh. 9. məyŋ əpni mylkiət
twmhare swpwrd kərta huŋ. 10. ləkɽioŋ ke ḍher ke ḍher zəmin
pər pəɽe the.

Exercise XXV

1. ys chaoni meŋ əṭhanve ghoɽe əwr sətais xəccər həyŋ.
2. bəndgaɽi ke lie do ṭəṭṭu zəruri həyŋ (cahieŋ). 3. hər admi
ke lie paŋc paŋc byghe əwr ek ek gae. 4. hər ek bəks meŋ koi
səw səw diasəlaiaŋ hoti həyŋ. 5. ek nəli mənjən tin ṭykiaŋ
sabwn əwr adh ser təmbaku ka tin lete aie. 6. ws ke caroŋ xərgoʃ
bhag gəe. 7. ṭokri meŋ chəy məchliaŋ həyn əwr mwṭṭhi bhər
nəmək. 8. voh dyn aega jəb (ky) twm log meri bat zərur
swnoge. 9. ws ka hər qədəm mən mən ka malum hota tha.

Exercise XXVI

1. yeh khet gol həy əwr voh mwrəbba, lekyn donoŋ ki sətəh
həmvar (bərabər) həy. 2. məydan ka phaṭək swbəh saɽhe nəw
bəje khwla hoga. 3. voh dəs bəje ʃam se soya rəha. 4. mwsafyr
səb se nəzdik abadi se pəndra kos dur the. 5. do servali
botəl thi lekin ws ka kag nəhiŋ tha. 6. yeh khet bəɽa əwr gol
həy, ws ka rəqba səva paŋc byghe həy. 7. ws ghoɽdəwɽ ka
məydan ys khet se bis bighe bəɽa həy. 8. ys kek ke lie pao
ser aṭa, mwṭṭhi bhər kyʃmyʃ, kwch məsale, əwr thoɽa dudh,
vəɣəyra zəruri hoga. 9. meri ghəɽi tez (ahysta) cəlti həy.
10. wn ki tadad dəs həy.

Exercise XXVII

1. məyŋ nəhiŋ aya kyoŋky kysi ne mwjhe nəhiŋ bwlaya.
2. do pəyhr ki top swnte hi həm rəvana hoŋge. 3. babu aj
afys (dəftər) meŋ aya—əgər nəhiŋ to kyoŋ nəhiŋ. 4. jəb ap
dhup meŋ bəyṭheŋ to ṭopi pəyhn lijie, nəhiŋ to sər meŋ dərd
hoga. 5. jəb am ka məwsəm pəwhŋcega to hər dyl meŋ xwʃi
hogi kyoŋky yeh phəl miṭha əwr rəsila həy. 6. ws ki avaz
swnte hi məyŋ ws ki tərəf dəwɽte dəwɽte həŋsa. 7. ləkhnəw
dekhne ke qabyl həy. 8. voh choṭa ləɽka ys kam ke layq
nəhiŋ hoga. 9. mere hwkm ke mwtabyq yeh kam kəro.
10. mwjrym qanun ke mwtabyq səza paega. 11. məyŋ yeh
cyk twmhare həvale (swpwrd) kəruŋga—jəb dyl cahe wse twɽao.
12. ys ylzam ke bare meŋ məyŋ kwch bəyan kəruŋ. 13. mere
nəzdik gəva(h) motəbər həy.

Exercise XXVIII

1. dəs dəs dəfa məyŋ ne ws se kəha. 2. kəi kəi sal tək meri əwr ws ki mwlaqat nəhiŋ hui. 3. geŋd sər ke upər upər gwzri. 4. bhəgoɽe ke sath sath dəwɽte hue ws ne ws ko axyr meŋ pəkəɽ lia. 5. ws ne jan bujhkər qəsd se yeh ʃərarət ki. 6. cəlie, dərya ke kynare kynare səyr kəreŋ əwr khel ke məydan tək pəwhŋceŋ jəhaŋ skul ke ləɽke krykəʈ khel rəhe hoŋge. 7. kləb ke nəwkər choʈi moʈi pəlʈən ki tərəh həyŋ. 8. mez pər kaɣəzoŋ ke ḍhər ke ḍher ləge hwe the. 9. age reŋgte reŋgte voh dwʃmən ki laynoŋ meŋ aŋkh bəcakər ghws gəe. 10. karobar əwr len den meŋ ws ki dyanətdari məʃhur thi. 11. voh həŋs həŋskər git ga rəha tha. 12. məyŋ ne bij bonevale ko bij bote hue dekha. 13. məyŋ ne ghur ghurkər dekha jəb tək ky meri əŋkheŋ thək nəhiŋ gəiŋ.

Exercise XXIX

1. kənjus əwr kyfayətʃyar ke dərmiyan zəmin o asman ka fərq hota həy. 2. dyn ba dyn bəcce ki taqət bəɽhti (jati) həy. 3. bəɣəyr yjazət ke koi əjayb-xane ya ehate meŋ bhi daxyl nəhiŋ ho səkta. 4. voh bedəm əwr bəɣəyr ʈopi ke peʃani se pəsina poŋchta hua pəwhŋca. 5. ys sənduqce meŋ kəm o beʃ do dərjən pynsyleŋ həyŋ. 6. voh bevəfa naynsaf əwr beiman admi həy; ys qədr bevəquf kəwn hoga jo ws ki bat mane (bat ka yəqin kəre). 7. dyanətdari zəmanasazi se kəhiŋ behtər həy. 8. aj kəl mwlk-e fars ko iran kəyhte həyŋ əwr ws ke rəyhne valoŋ ko irani kəyhte həyŋ. 9. surəj ɣərib əwr əmir pər yəksaŋ cəməkta həy. 10. yeh ʃəyhtir zyadəh se zyadah bis fwʈ ləmba hoga, ʃayəd kwch kəm ho. 11. ws ne yeh məjbur hokər kia (ws ko yeh məjburən kərna pəɽa).